The following endorsements are [generous enough to read this bo] *generous enough to read this bo* *I wrote. They are wives, mothers, students, sisters,* *all—they are daughters of a good God who gives rest to those* *He loves. They've gone before you in this work, and they—like* *me—are cheering you on.*

◇◇◇◇◇◇

"Accepting fatigue and living a frenzied life is not God's best for you and me. Not only will this book change the language with which we describe the problem, it will deliver a clear path through your current struggle and to the deeper rest and fuller life God has promised to give us. Thank you, Jess, for moving our mindset on the topic of resting and living fully awake; our generation is more whole for it."

Oghogho Tayo

"This journey is worth it! Our first calling is to be God's beloved, and we get to walk in the fullness of that inheritance. We are off the hook. The weight of the whole world does not rest on our shoulders. Learning how to recover and live from a place of rest is one of the most powerful acts of worship you'll ever experience."

Ellery Sadler

"I see a profound fatigue in myself, my friends, and my patients these days that is deeper than what science and medicine can cure. As Peter said to Jesus, our Messiah holds the words of life, and Jess ushers these words of life to our weary souls in these pages. Living fully awake is a principle that has refreshed my days and is breathing new vigor into my walk with Jesus. This book is a must-read."

Kristin Kirkland, MD, MPH

"Once again Jess has written a life-giving book that is relevant and real while also being convicting and challenging in the very best way. Thank you, Jess, for speaking to my soul and offering practical steps to the true rhythm of rest."

Lanessa Amburgey

"Jess is the real deal! She practices what she preaches, and having seen this process lived out just shows that it can work and provide so much life-giving freedom in Christ!"

Heather Gage

"This book is rich with practical ways to fight against our weariness in all areas of our lives. I love Jess's approach to this topic, as she addresses all the ways we can be (and are!) tired. Perfect for any and every woman!"

Sybil K.

"This book is going to be your go-to how-to guide for living fully awake for the days ahead. Jess has such an honest way of talking about real-life things while also bringing biblical truth and practical application to your 'next steps' plan. Buy more than one copy because you're going to want to hand one to your girlfriends too."

Tam Odom

"All of Jess's books have inspired me, but this one resonated on a new level. Her real talk about resetting our life rhythms to embrace God's gift of rest was both inviting and challenging to me as a lifelong doer! Her personal insights and practical applications awakened me to the truth that God *gives* rest to those He loves, and He loves me (and you)! As we constantly fight fatigue on the battleground of our daily lives, Jess's words remind us that God's rest is a precious gift to be received and enjoyed—not earned—for our good and for His glory! Sign me up for the 'Awake Women's Club'! I'll see you there!"

Victoria Stewart Malone

"We live in a culture that tends to see lack of margin and being overwhelmed and tired as a badge of honor, but this view doesn't reflect God's design. In *Tired of Being Tired*, Jess writes to the reader as a friend, speaks to our need for rest with authority and grace, and challenges us to implement healthier life rhythms. It's time to stop seeing rest as passive or lazy and start embracing it as a gift from God that is for our good."

Aleah Dixon

tired of being tired

RECEIVE GOD'S REALISTIC REST
FOR YOUR SOUL-DEEP EXHAUSTION

Jess Connolly

BakerBooks

a division of Baker Publishing Group
Grand Rapids, Michigan

Published by Baker Books
a division of Baker Publishing Group
Grand Rapids, Michigan
BakerBooks.com

Printed in the United States of America

Library of Congress Cataloging-in-Publication Data
Names: Connolly, Jess, author.
Title: Tired of being tired : receive God's realistic rest for your soul-deep exhaustion / Jess Connolly.
Description: Grand Rapids, Michigan : Baker Books, a division of Baker Publishing Group, [2024] | Includes bibliographical references.
Identifiers: LCCN 2023029609 | ISBN 9781540902504 (paper) | ISBN 9781540903945 (casebound) | ISBN 9781493444885 (ebook)
Subjects: LCSH: Christian women—Religious life. | Fatigue. | Women—Health and hygiene.
Classification: LCC BV4527 .C643955 2024 | DDC 248.8/43—dc23/eng/20230906
LC record available at https://lccn.loc.gov/2023029609

The author is represented by Illuminate Literary Agency, www.IlluminateLiterary.com.

Baker Publishing Group publications use paper produced from sustainable forestry practices and postconsumer waste whenever possible.

24   25   26   27   28   29   30   7   6   5   4   3   2   1

For Anna, Henslee, Caroline, Emily, Liz, and Nicci.
We got to come and see + go and tell.

contents

author's note

A lot of writing a book can be lonely. You're sitting in a room or a coffee shop, by yourself, tapping out words that you hope will serve people—hoping they hit hearts in ways they're meant to, hoping you're not alone in what you're feeling. I was incredibly grateful to have a handful of women who agreed to read this book as I wrote it and give live feedback—not only to me but by adding their words and thoughts to this book as well.

I call them the midwives of this book, as they prayed for both me and you, knowing we would all collectively fight fatigue in these pages. I'm honored to share their names below, and it's their endorsements you just read when you opened this book. In the coming chapters, you may see a quick excerpt pop up from some of them in the "What Women Have to Say" sections. But know that whether you're seeing a direct quote of theirs or not, their hands, hearts, and stories are all over this book.

Introducing the midwives of this book:

Aleah Dixon   Erin Anspach
Lanessa Amburgey   Gianna
Tam Odom   Evonne Heredia

Victoria Stewart Malone   Morgan Strehlow

Alexa I.   Sybil K.

Rachel Sweatt   Nicole Smith

Jessie Hood   Ellery Frost

Kristin Kirkland, MD, MPH   Megan Renck

Setareh Campion   Natalie McPheron

DeAnna Allen   Makayla

Chloé Minyon   Giovanna

Brittany Pomeroy   Brittany Estes

Rachel Johnston   Heather Gage

Nicole Gillette   Jennifer Brown-Carpenter

Kerry Scheidegger   Oghogho Tayo

Thank you, friends.

one

our exhaustion runs deep

Every woman I know is tired.

In all the seasons, they're exhausted. Whether their kids are little or old, whether they work in the home or outside of it as well, every mom I know is exhausted. My friends who just graduated from college—they're tired. The newly empty nesters who thought their season of sleepless nights was gone forever—they're still expressing fatigue. Every woman I know is tired.

It comes out in different ways. We blink back tired tears when a friend asks us how we're doing. We swallow deep sighs in the morning in disbelief that the night is already over. We watch social media wistfully, wondering how she gets to go on so many vacations. *It must be nice*, we think. We start to feel the anxiety rising as the weekend winds down and the "Sunday Scaries" start in earnest.

We make jokes about how we'll get sleep when we're dead. We promise ourselves that it will probably get better after the next deadline, the next month, the next event, or the next season.

But it's not getting better.

The question is, Are we tired enough to change our minds? Tired enough to change our lives? Tired enough to ask honest questions about how we got here and how we get out of this cycle of exhaustion?

We Inherited This Exhaustion

I come from an incredible line of women, though there's one part of our heritage that I could have done without: We're not sleepers.

I thought I'd escaped the curse because in my teens and early twenties I could fall asleep anywhere. Honestly, I can still fall asleep anywhere. But stay asleep? That's an elusive pipe dream, a miraculous ship that sailed swiftly away from me right around the time I had my last kid.

I grew up knowing my mom didn't sleep. I'd see her bedroom light on in the middle of the night or notice the telltale signs in the morning: a mug, a book, a scribbled-in journal, all haphazardly placed near a chair after she'd crawled out of bed in the wee hours. She never complained. She wouldn't even say she didn't sleep well. We just knew that she'd been up for hours.

So, when the sleeplessness started for me, I accepted it and set out to redeem the time. I'd pray quietly in bed, grateful that at least my body was getting rest. I'd scroll on my phone, make lists, or shop online, putting things that I'd never buy in a cart on an app but thinking, *A girl can dream! If I can't actually dream, I can "dream shop."*

On the worst nights, when sleep wouldn't come, I'd try to slip out of bed without waking up my husband, gently tug my favorite blanket from beneath the sheets, and head to the living room to start the day. I'd do just as my mother had done: read the Bible, journal, and eventually pull out my laptop and start working. I didn't complain—or at least I tried hard not to—as the family began waking up at reasonable times. This was my birthright. This was just the way it was.

But everything shifted one spring when I was thirty-seven years old, and the occasional night of sleeplessness turned into long, agonizing stretches of insomnia. Honestly, it would have been a different story if it had just been insomnia. But instead, it was insomnia caused by anxiety: rolling panic attacks that would start when I lay down to sleep and wouldn't subside until the sun came up.

For me, it would start with one unfinished task or an errant thought about something I hadn't done well. Then that little ember would catch flame in my mind, growing and throwing out other embers of ideas: tasks for the next day, unsolvable problems, deep spiritual questions, and a gnawing sense of dread about how dependent other people were on me. If you've struggled with sleeplessness, you know the fire that rages when the clock changes and you imagine the entire next day on four hours of sleep, on three . . . OK, on just two.

I'd lie there trying to take deep breaths, desperately attempting to douse my anxious thoughts with prayers, until it felt like my entire body was burning with fear. But all the while I would know in my gut, exhaustion had burned through the physical part of my being and was now smoldering in my spirit, mind, and emotions.

I was also learning that my spiritual problems had a way of becoming physical problems when left unattended. My unseen fatigue was becoming visible and unavoidable.

I can't say that season came out of nowhere because I've chased down the root cause, and I'll share it with you soon. But I can tell you that one stormy night turned into two tough nights that rolled into a cluster of weeks and months when I barely recognized myself.

I was honestly relieved when morning hit. It meant that the worst of it was over. But I'd have to somehow make it through the blurry, teary day praying that no one would ask me how I was doing.

Because I was so tired.

And I was tired not only because I hadn't slept. This fatigue was now rooted in every facet of my being: my soul, my mind, my heart, and my body.

That's the problem with exhaustion: It always wants more. It permeates every facet of our life until we address the source of our fatigue.

As for me, I was tired from picking myself up and speaking truth against a barrage of spiritual lies.

I was tired from just trying to get through the next few weeks, when relief never seemed to come.

I was tired from trying to obey and please God.

I was tired from being everything to everyone.

I was tired from showing up when others didn't.

I was tired from serving, cleaning, leading, and loving with my whole body.

I was tired from the mental gymnastics it took to get myself and our family through the day, from the appointments to the meal plans to the extracurriculars and beyond.

I was tired from answering existential questions for others, never even being able to make it to my own.

I was tired from multitasking every stinking minute of every exhausting day.

I was tired from the pent-up emotions that threatened to leak out if I had a moment alone.

I was tired from the trauma of my past peeking out behind everyday interactions.

I was tired from processing all the things so I could stay present and be a kind human.

And even though I'd read every book on rest that I could get my hands on, even though I was seeing a spiritual director, even though I took a weekly day off, even though I exercised and moved my body and drank green smoothies—I was so ridiculously tired.

But what could I do? I got out of bed, washed my face, iced my dark circles, made a cup of coffee, put on fresh clothes, and tried again. Only to dread coming face-to-face with the soul-tired, sleepless night that would await me again in a few hours.

We are certainly not the first generation to fight fatigue, as all the tendencies and tensions that keep us living tired have been building for centuries. We inherited this exhaustion collectively, no matter how well our mothers slept.

You're Tired Too

In the name of Jesus, I pray you don't have sleepless night after night and days of try, try, trying again.

I pray that your exhaustion hasn't exploded into anxiety-stricken hours that leave your body feeling inflamed and beaten up.

But chances are, you're pretty tired too.

I mean, I can guess that you're tired because you opened this book. But truly, we women are a tired people.

Unfortunately, we have grown to accept exhaustion as our reality, we've learned to wear our busyness as a badge of honor, and our fatigue is the assumptive price we pay for being a woman.

You may have heard about a pay-equity gap. That's where men are consistently paid more for the same jobs that women do. Did you know that researchers have now confirmed what most of us already expected? There is also a gender exhaustion gap. Statistically, women are almost 20 percent more likely to experience fatigue and burnout than men.[1]

Two out of three women say they don't just feel tired—they've reached a state of burnout. That statistic gets much higher among women in the twenty-four-to-thirty-four-year-old range. And the research shows that we're more tired not because we're weaker or less resilient; rather, we're just more likely to assume responsibility in multiple spheres: physically, emotionally, and mentally.

You haven't been imagining it; women are 1.5 times more likely than men to wake up not feeling rested (from roughly the same amount of sleep). When asked to unpack this data, Dr. Seema Khosla, the doctor who found this information, cited the "incredible amount of pressure that some women feel" and said, "We need to put away our superhero capes."[2]

And in case you're wondering, or maybe you already had a hunch, living through a global pandemic ravaged our already fragile relationship with fatigue and mental health as women. Now one out of every two women says she's dealing with some form of anxiety and notable tiredness.

You and I, we're smart women. We know when something is up, when there's something fishy going on.

So often shame has led us to believe this is *our* problem and that something is wrong with us because we can't seem to figure it out. Instead of feeling grieved over our exhaustion and using our energy to fight our fatigue, we've felt ashamed, and that has kept us from figuring out its root cause.

I feel like I'm tired because I've taken on more than I should have. I believe I'm tired because I'm not as strong as the women around me. I think that maybe I'm tired because my rhythms or boundaries are off. I feel like I'm tired because I scroll on my phone instead of sleeping. I could be tired because of my autoimmune disease, my kids, and the deadline that's coming up.

But my friends who are tired—I certainly don't feel like their fatigue is their fault.

My friend Lindsay doesn't have anxiety-ridden sleepless nights like me, but she's mothering a medically fragile child who needs round-the-clock care. My coworker Emily isn't a wife or a mom, but balancing multiple freelance clients to build her career leaves her feeling like she has to burn the candle at both ends. Another friend, Anne, is an empty nester who thought she'd be in a season of rest by now but finds herself watching her grandkids almost full-time. She doesn't want to live a tired life, but she does want to show up for her family—how in the world is she supposed to pursue both?

Are single moms to blame for how tired they are? Should college-aged girls feel shame about the pace that's expected of them to perform and live up to the pressure they feel? When you think back to the past seasons of your life and see your own fatigue, is your assumption that it's all your fault?

Looking at all this data and taking a step back, maybe you and I can put our very wise heads together, use the power of the Spirit that raised Jesus Christ from the grave, and ask some important questions:

Why is the enemy of our souls targeting the energy of women?

Why is every woman we know experiencing fatigue on a deep soul level?

What if the guilt cycle we get stuck in about our own exhaustion is a ploy to keep us from figuring out what is truly fatiguing us?

What will happen if we start to look at this from a spiritual, practical, and realistic perspective? Why are we so tired? How did we get this way? What does God say about it and what will actually help?

What if we throw down our cups of coffee (theoretically—don't break that mug; it's cute) and scream, "No more!"? We're tired of saying we're tired. We're tired of being tired. We're tired of feeling tired.

Jesus didn't purchase our freedom for a life of fatigue, so there has got to be more than an endless cycle of exhaustion.

This is actually a cultural problem that demands a spiritual and practical answer.

We are soul-tired because we're coming against a culture of reactive defeat, one that assumes exhaustion is inevitable instead of fighting for rest. We idolize busyness over a sustainable pace and reward women for pushing through rather than blessing our God-given boundaries.

Finding soul rest will take fighting the defeated acceptance that it will always be this way, tearing down the idols of busyness and hustle, and learning our own unique needs for renewal while we obediently create rhythms for a sustainable pace.

We want the free-and-light life that our Friend and Savior promised us in Matthew 11.

Are you tired? Worn out? Burned out on religion? Come to me. Get away with me and you'll recover your life. I'll show you how to take a real rest. Walk with me and work with me—watch how

I do it. Learn the unforced rhythms of grace. I won't lay anything heavy or ill-fitting on you. Keep company with me and you'll learn to live freely and lightly. (vv. 28–30 MSG)

We are tired of being tired. And we're ready to live.

Are you riled up? I kind of hope so. Because I sure am.

Feeling guilty about being tired is not helping us. Reading books written by people who don't understand our pain points or our lives exacerbates the issue. Trying to "let go and let God" and "just not worry about it" is not easing the deep soul issue that stirs up our fatigue.

I believe that for us to feel better, see lasting change, and experience healing at the point of our true exhaustion, we're going to need to get a little feisty.

But what if you're too tired to fight? What if you just need help because your body, soul, and mind are all yawning and threatening to shut down completely? I'll volunteer to be the fired-up friend who fights with you and for you.

Hi, My Name Is Jess, and I Am Not Sweet

My life is not precious. Or gentle. Or quiet.

I have a husband and four kids—three of whom are teenagers. None of my kids are sweet. They're loving! They're kind! But they're not quiet kids, which they come by honestly. Their dad and I met in high school, where we quickly determined that we wanted to leave the world more in awe of God than we found it, and we've been about that life for the last twenty years.

He's a vision caster, a wide-eyed apostolic dreamer who builds things out of nothing and won't quit until whatever he's working on is really good, whether it's loading the dishwasher correctly or building a community that shines the light of Jesus in a dark world.

I'm a passionate coach who wants everyone to keep moving toward what God has called them to; I hate defeat and love change.

I don't know when to leave well enough alone, whether I'm helping women step into their calling or getting my kids to do their chores.

We lead a church, small in stature at currently 150 people but large in heart and vision. We're out to see the renewal of the American church, and we're starting here in Charleston, South Carolina. We live in the heart of downtown, where people experiencing homelessness stop by, sirens often wail, partyers puke in our yard, and the door is a revolving portal for the people in our church.

I lead a team of women in my small business, Go + Tell Gals, where we equip and encourage women all over the world. We coach women and certify other coaches in our process, and we love what we do—so we sometimes have a hard time putting it down. On top of our beautiful spiritual impact, it's rarely lost on me that multiple people's incomes are dependent on my work. And hundreds of women's callings are wrapped up in me fighting for them, affirming their gifts, training them, and . . . working.

What I'm not doing is boasting about all this. Because if I'm candid with you, I'm rarely proud of how much I hold in life and often somewhat embarrassed about it.

I feel shame, just like the next gal, about how I bite off more than I can chew, whether that's with my kids or my calling or just saying yes to things I have no business saying yes to.

But what's most important to me is that you have an adequate picture of my life as I fight with you and for you in the pages ahead: I'm not sweet, and my life isn't quiet.

I tell you this openly because I want you to know that a vision for realistic rest only works if it works for all of us. I believe that God offers His abundant gift of rest to all of us, and I don't believe receiving this rest presupposes that we live sweet and tidy lives where everything always fits and works perfectly.

I'm not going to advocate that you go on a silent retreat to get your soul back because I know that's honestly not realistic for most of us. I'm also not going to advocate for that because I'm the gal who watches TV in the shower, and I feel great about it.

(Some people like to be alone with their thoughts; I want to watch *The West Wing*.)

I'd be a fraud if I pitched you a hushed life of soft fabrics and muted noises. I've got a feeling that your life is often loud too, whether it's people or feelings or due dates or existential pressures that are screaming at you every second.

If all of us lived tame and underwhelming lives, we might not be so tired—but we also wouldn't be human.

You and I need honest words about the state of our exhausted souls. We're desperate for the transparency of other women who are just as tired as we are, and we need realistic and fruitful truth from Scripture to help us fight this fatigue.

We don't need another person putting advice on our shoulders who doesn't understand our circumstances or refuses to acknowledge that we're up against a different fight than they are.

We don't need any more guilt or shame about how we got here. We just need honest answers about how to move forward.

We are tired, but we don't have to stay this way. Together we're going to do some diagnostic work to find the true source of our fatigue. We'll go to God's Word to find realistic kingdom approaches to rest. And finally, we'll implement sustainable spiritual rhythms into our lives that leave us refreshed for the rest of our lives.

If you're tired of being tired, if the cycle of exhaustion is no longer serving you, let's move forward together. Amen?

Reflection Questions

1. Do you know women in your similar life stage who seem rested? What seems to be their secret?
2. Why do you think you're as tired as you are?
3. What's your honest response to Jesus's words from Matthew 11?

Low Power Mode

If you have an iPhone, you're probably familiar with Low Power Mode. When your battery hits 20 percent or lower, a notification will pop up asking if you'd like to switch to Low Power Mode. Once your phone is in this mode, it uses less of the battery in order to conserve your power longer, but it also internally powers down a little—by not using its full capabilities.

You can't really tell from the outside, as a user, that the phone is in Low Power Mode. But internally, it's doing less and saving up.

In several chapters of this book, I'll give you some Low Power Mode suggestions to fight the different types of exhaustion. These ideas will be small, practical ways you can conserve your precious energy and hopefully feel a little less tired right where you're at.

We'll kick it off easy for the first chapter:

Notice anytime you feel shame about your fatigue. Conserve some of your precious spiritual, physical, mental, or emotional energy by reminding yourself that feeling tired is not a problem you caused. You did not start this fight.

two

it will get worse
if it doesn't get better

My knees tell the story of a semi-clumsy girl.

While I wasn't all that outdoorsy as a kid (and still am not), I constantly had scrapes or healing scabs on one or both knees. I was the queen of tripping on sidewalks, falling up steps, and taking a tumble for no good reason.

I've got multiple scars on both knees, but the worst one is on my right leg. The injury took off the pigment in my skin, so the oblong scar is completely white; it doesn't tan or burn. In the summer, it stands out against the rest of my leg like a large white dot. I feel like it gives my body some character, so I don't hate it, but it's funny because it's the least dramatic story with the worst-looking scar.

That wound came just a few years ago on a summer day that was so hot. We escaped to the water with the kids, hoping the wind and waves would bring a little solace. Unfortunately, even the beach was too hot, and the kids were fussy, so we didn't stay long. After schlepping all our stuff to the sand and discovering we couldn't stay, we started schlepping it back to the car.

My husband, Nick, led the march back to the parking lot while I followed up behind the kids with the final load. And at one point, with the air hazy from heat and my body probably dehydrated, dragging a cooler and a beach bag full of sunscreen—I dropped.

It wasn't a full-on faint; I didn't collapse. But I didn't trip either. Maybe I got light-headed, or maybe my body needed a break. I'm not sure. Whatever the cause, the effect was that my knees bent down to the hot sand, and I dropped everything I had been dragging. It was so subtle that no one ahead of me even noticed. It wasn't until I got to the car that Nick pointed down at my knee and we realized that some combination of the sand and the heat hitting my skin had burned it clear off. And, of course, later we'd recognize the pigment had gone with it.

Sometimes the fall you don't see coming, the one that seems the least dramatic, leaves the biggest scar.

As I look back on the last few years of my life, I can see that I've been taking tumbles toward exhaustion for the long haul. And I realize now that if you don't stop to tend to the problem, it will add up. It will get worse before it gets better.

Sometimes it's a little tumble. For example, I might find myself crying in unexpected places after a busy few weeks as I wipe my face and apologize to the (almost always) unlikely recipient of my tears. Or maybe I say yes to too much, convinced that future me will be more organized and capable. And then panic comes in the messy present, and I end up profusely apologizing as I cancel as much as possible. Or I scream at my kids for something minor just because I'm so done and overwhelmed. These feel like little tumbles of tiredness: I pick myself up, dust my knees off, and try again the next day.

But some years ago, I experienced my first significant fall with fatigue.

I'd just finished the edits on my first book; my kids were eight, seven, six, and two. Our other baby—our church plant—was one year old, and like most one-year-olds, it was fussy, hands-on, and making messes as it found its feet. My online print shop had a team of three women, and the profits from our sales funded three church plants: ours in Charleston, one in Pakistan, and one in Amsterdam.

In that season, I hadn't yet reconciled that I was a working mom. I was convinced I could be the "room mom" in all the elementary classes, be present for every nap-time cuddle, and make every meal. I wanted to be everything to everyone, and I wanted to make it all work.

Spoiler alert: Wanting to be everything to everyone is often the preamble to a breakdown of epic proportions.

I had also just begun to travel to teach and preach at conferences, which felt like a great way to use my God-given gifts and empower other women. But because I didn't love being away from my kids, I'd load up on family time before and after being away, trying desperately to make sure that no one felt my absence, that no one else paid for me stepping into my calling. You can imagine who did pay in the end.

What really tripped me up was that I wasn't trying to be all things for the approval of others; rather, it was because of my recognition that *everything* mattered. I was driven by a deep-seated belief that my work was important, my family was necessary, and for me to steward it well—I had to do it all. I had this much right: Yes, all of it mattered deeply! But it wasn't all on me, and I was struggling because I believed the subtle lie that it was. People needed the finances from our business; they needed their salaries . . . so I had to keep pushing. My kids needed a loving, present mom . . . so I had to keep pushing. Our church needed attention, care, prayer, and shepherding . . . so I had to keep pushing.

There weren't a lot of warning signs, but if I'm honest, there also wasn't anyone telling me, "You don't have to do it all." Because I didn't express my exhaustion and because I was working under the assumption that if it was hard, it was my fault, no one knew I was struggling.

Pretending you can handle everything, even when you're exhausted, is the surest way to burn out fast.

I was away at a speaking event one weekend when I noticed a pretty gruesome headache coming on. I carried ibuprofen with me for just this sort of thing—the overwhelm of people and pace, which often caused me pain—and started popping them like candy. The medicine didn't touch it, but I figured it was the conference food and lack of sleep. I was scheduled to speak on the last day of the event. Still, I wanted to be helpful the entire time, so I organized a group run with some women I met online and even did a little headstand tutorial with dozens of women on the grass of the retreat center. I popped a few more ibuprofen.

By the day I was scheduled to speak, I could barely tolerate light or sound, and my roommate at the event was another speaker doing as much as she could to take care of me. The hour before I spoke, I was laid out on the uncomfy conference-center bed as she did my makeup—I wanted to exert as little energy as possible to do my job well. Finally, I mustered up the energy to get onstage, preached my little heart out, winced through the pain as I prayed for women after the message, and then walked back to the room to collapse before I caught my early flight the following day.

In the middle of the night, I knew something was seriously wrong. This wasn't a migraine—was it a tumor? Was I dying? Is this how I went out? Away from my kids at a women's conference?

I don't remember traveling home. I know there was a shuttle van to the airport. I remember falling asleep in the back row, but I don't remember getting on the plane or getting picked up at my home airport. My husband and I pretended it might get better if I got to my space, bed, and everyday foods. I don't remember most of the next three days—there was a drive to urgent care for a shot of some serious painkiller. We were still working under the assumption that this was a migraine, even though I'd never had one in my life.

I remember waking up and vomiting from pain a few hours after the shot, a second drive to urgent care, and then the emergency room. Doctors in and out running tests, my husband holding my hand, and my mom rushing in during the middle of a spinal tap. Then I remember my mom finding out that a student at the teaching hospital was doing my spinal tap and hearing her voice demanding that a student not be the one sticking a needle into my spine. Shortly after that, things got rushed and wild and frantic.

My spinal tap revealed meningitis, and since my headache had begun days earlier, I was at risk for stroke, brain damage, and a long list of horrific side effects. No matter what, I was looking at an intense hospital stay and a long road to recovery.

I was devastated and embarrassed that my exhaustion and weakened immune system had caused this hardship for everyone else. My husband was now juggling all four kids and coming to visit me in the hospital, and the event organizers were nervous about who I might have infected. I had to cancel a speaking event for the next month, and I hated letting them down. I was grieved about the problems I'd caused, but unfortunately, I didn't take this colossal stumble and make any significant life changes—yet. It could have been the moment that changed everything, and I wish it would have been.

Sadly, instead of slowing down, I doubled down. I remember going "live" online to my followers from the hospital bed with an insight I'd read in my Bible through blurry vision that morning. I remember crying to my doctor, convincing him I needed to be released early to return to my kids. I remember the first time I tried to work out again, way too soon, only to have my body crumple on the yoga mat in my bedroom from the leftover searing pain.

Looking back, I have so much compassion for that woman desperate to keep going. She was convinced that she was the problem, that she'd let everyone down with her weakness, and that her fatigue was a failure.

I was still buying the lie that I had to push through, that somehow exhaustion was a badge of honor, and that this was just the way it was. I thought the constant fatigue might get better in a different season. I wasn't ready to change my life to experience life change.

This tumble, this terrific fall, wasn't my last. Because this is the truth about being tired: It will get worse if it doesn't get better.

Realistic Rest Could Be the Answer

There are thousands of terrifying stories about people who didn't rest and how it cost them. And I wish I had equally remarkable stories about a time when I rested and then conquered the world. Or I could tell you about some heroes of the faith and how they withdrew to find their souls.

But I promise to be ruthlessly honest with you and refuse to sell you a false bill of goods about a sweet and slow life that's unrealistic for us. So, here's the truth: There aren't a lot of sexy stories about wild, life-changing rest. And here's one reason why: We won't experience real, lasting, eternal rest here on earth.

The bad news is that while we live under the effects of a fallen world and experience the pain and tension of corruptible bodies, we will always long for the complete recreation and blissful peace that heaven promises us.

The good news is that we can stop feeling shame about our fatigue and learn to live within the boundaries and limits of our human bodies while we eagerly look forward to the renewal and rest of eternity.

We will always crave heaven-sized rest in our human bodies, but we will always be left wanting more.

My husband has a rule at our church, Bright City, that no one can hang signs that read WELCOME HOME within the building. This trend became popular a few years ago, and maybe your church has these signs (no judgment from me—I think they're cute), but Nick is vehemently opposed. He reasons that he never wants anyone who steps foot in our space to confuse our church with home. As he often reminds me, heaven is our home. And while the church is an incredible expression of the kingdom here on earth, it's still a dimly lit reflection of a beautiful reality that awaits us.

The same is true for rest on earth and rest in eternity.

I know that it will get worse if you and I don't adjust our pace and rhythms and readjust what we believe we're responsible for. Our bodies will continue to break under the weight of the spiritual, physical, mental, and emotional exhaustion we've grown accustomed to. Our relationships will suffer: with God, with one another, and most assuredly with ourselves. We won't recognize who we are or how we got here. We'll buckle under the weight of anxiety and overwhelm, and stress will seep into every pore of our bodies until inflammation, fatigue, defeat, and depression are the norm.

It will get worse if it doesn't get better, and I won't sell you a lie about what better looks like.

Let's Learn from Elijah

In 1 Kings 19, we encounter the prophet Elijah at the end of his actual rope. I'll give him a lot of credit and remind you from the get-go that he was serving God in unusual times and difficult circumstances. God had commanded Elijah to prophesy and announce a terrible drought in the land. Still, as it typically goes for prophets, Elijah also had to experience the hardship of that pronunciation. God continually provided for him, but it was often in miraculous last-second saves. To be blunt, I find it incredibly exhausting rereading the Scripture about his ministry. There were wildly high highs and defeating and terrifyingly low lows.

In one of those lows, Elijah was being threatened and chased, and he became exhausted and discouraged.

> Elijah was afraid and ran for his life. When he came to Beersheba in Judah, he left his servant there while he himself went a day's journey into the wilderness. He came to a broom bush, sat down under it and prayed that he might die. "I have had enough, LORD," he said. "Take my life; I am no better than my ancestors." Then he lay down under the bush and fell asleep.

All at once an angel touched him and said, "Get up and eat." He looked around, and there by his head was some bread baked over hot coals, and a jar of water. He ate and drank and then lay down again.

The angel of the LORD came back a second time and touched him and said, "Get up and eat, for the journey is too much for you." So he got up and ate and drank. Strengthened by that food, he traveled forty days and forty nights until he reached Horeb, the mountain of God. There he went into a cave and spent the night. (1 Kings 19:3–9)

I want to note a few things here and invite us to apply the same wisdom to our lives.

First, Elijah was afraid because he was being threatened. He was being pursued, and he was discouraged about his circumstances and, I'd imagine, the spiritual plight of everyone he was supposed to be leading toward God's truth. His feelings were justified. And if you're exhausted and discouraged, I have a hunch that yours are too. Elijah wasn't weak; he was human. You aren't the problem because you can't carry the weight of the world; the fallenness of humanity and the pace of our culture are the predicament.

Second, I cannot be more grateful that the angel of the Lord who ministers to Elijah gives it to him straight about what's next: *It's too much for you. But, to be honest, it's too much for anyone!* In the chapter before, Elijah had just battled 450 prophets of Baal. That story is wild, and it goes in Elijah's favor—but not without a fight. King Ahab, the ruler of the time, believes this prophet Elijah is stirring up trouble for his people. This is mostly because Elijah is speaking against the false god Baal and all of his prophets. To prove God's worthiness, Elijah battles Baal's 450 false prophets in a duel of sorts: Whoever's God supernaturally sets a sacrificial bull on fire first wins. And to up the ante, Elijah says he'll pour water on his altar to give him an extra-unfair advantage. So, we've got 400-plus prophets crying out to Baal for fire on a dry altar versus Elijah, alone, asking the God of his ancestors to light a wet altar on fire.

God wins. The false prophets are seized. Elijah is vindicated but, we can only imagine, exhausted.

Even when we're in the right spot, even when we're working on behalf of the Lord, even when we're being obedient to His call, exhaustion is going to come.

I wonder what it would look like if you and I began to view accepting God's gift of rest here on this earth as His compassionate and merciful condolence for that which is too much for us.

Our Father doesn't give us rest to be cute; He gives us rest because *we need it*. He gives us rest because He is wildly compassionate to His children who live under the effects of a fallen world. If you have carried shame about feeling fatigue, in the name of Jesus, now is the time to get rid of it. You don't need rest because you're weak; you need rest because this life is too much—at best. Which is why our fully human, fully God Friend and Savior also hit moments of exhaustion on earth. It's a condition of being alive, of being a human in the now-and-not-yet kingdom of God.

I'm not being dramatic when I say that parenting teens is too much for me. Sitting through scary board meetings where huge financial decisions are being made is too much for me. Consistently losing sleep when caring for a newborn is too much for anybody. Serving our ailing parents as they pass from this life to the next is too much. Processing the monotony of the Monday-through-Friday consistent grind is too much. Healing from generational trauma, broken relationships, and every single wound that the culture around us inflicts on us—it's all too much.

This side of heaven, rest will never be a one-and-done cure-all. But it will be our ongoing practice and gift to receive from God, who always meets us in our weariest places. God says it Himself, and it's time you hear it from Him: The journey is too much for you. Too much for you to go it alone. So don't—receive the gift of realistic rest God continually offers us.

If you take nothing else from Elijah's story, I hope you take this: Your need for rest in the face of the too-muchness of your own life is not weak; it's a need that your Father wants to meet. But continually ignoring that need will not leave you feeling equipped; it just might lead you to quit. This is a prime example of why the push-through mentality of our tired culture is not serving us or making us any stronger.

I don't know what will happen in your life after you embrace realistic, biblical, lasting rhythms of rest. But here's what could happen:

Things could get better.

You could feel more connected to God as your Father, Friend, and daily Companion.

You could feel at home in your body, at peace with your own pace.

You might understand the gospel better, the good gift you've been given to set you free.

You might have a better understanding of your purpose and place in the kingdom.

You could see what your body feels like when you're not always exhausted.

You might feel freer when you stop trying to be everything to everyone.

There's a chance you could experience healing from over-responsibility and imposter syndrome.

I believe you might get a handle on your mental health if you begin to rest.

Your mind might feel easier to quiet and your thoughts more manageable to process.

You could experience the peace that passes understanding, even amid chaos.

If you began to rest consistently and realistically, you could feel more whole emotionally.

You could feel your feelings and live less distracted and compartmentalized.

You could feel capable of encountering great and hard days with your emotions as a help, not a hindrance.

Your spiritual, physical, mental, and emotional well-being could improve if you embrace rest—but they will absolutely all get worse if you don't.

But I've staked my life on the truth of God's Word, and I've found it to be true. And He's got a boatload of promises that are ours for the taking if we will receive the rest He's offering. More than that, I've seen the empirical evidence in my life and others' that if we keep running forward exhausted—it will get worse.

So, what do you say? Should we keep going? See what God might have for us together?

I'm in if you are.

I asked seventy brave and generous women to read the chapters of this book as I was writing them and give feedback and insight in real time. I cannot thank them enough for how they've helped craft this message. But in regard to this chapter, one kind reader asked me, "Will it really get worse? Isn't there a possibility that things could just stay the same? I could just stay tired for the rest of my life?"

I feel like this question was not only honest but also courageous—because so many of us probably would settle for things staying the same.

But this is where I'd love to put on my coaching hat and just give you the honest news: No, things can't just stay the same. Because physical, spiritual, mental, and emotional exhaustion wears you down until you feel less capable and less connected to God. Things cannot possibly just stay the same because the pace of our lives will only move faster as technology and culture increase and grow. We are not static beings; we cannot just stay the same.

So, in love, I want to come alongside you and say, your fight against tired *will* get worse, but it could get better. Finding the source of your fatigue and embracing realistic rhythms of rest will help you when you feel like it's all too much.

three

why we resist rest

You can basically sell me anything.

I love a good pitch about how a product is going to change my life, and *I buy it*. I buy the pitch and the thing I probably don't need. I'm a sucker for a good commercial or an Instagram ad, and I've been known to make large life decisions inspired by billboards.

This is the kind of friend I am: If you and I are having coffee and you're telling me about a new book that you're only two chapters into, I buy it. While you're still talking. Maybe I will get the audio version and listen to the same two chapters before I even get back to my house. If you like it, or even think you like it, I want to try it.

But by the grace of God and for the sake of our bank account, I'm married to a skeptic. He taught me how to read website product reviews, and now I use them religiously. He researches and considers every option before making any kind of decision, and his caution has influenced me to pump the brakes a few times before cosigning on every product, idea, trip, or life change with enthusiastic abandon.

And what do you know? My adoption of his healthy skepticism has changed the game for me. Now when I commit to something, whether it's a book or a candle or a parenting strategy, I'm making an informed and confident choice.

So, this one is for the skeptics, the cautious, and the informed decision makers.

You and I both know you're tired.

We both agree that it will get worse if it doesn't get better.

But what about all the reasons why you're not resting now? What is different about this book from the thousands of others you could choose from? What if I don't understand your specific life demands, concerns, fears, and hang-ups with living a more rested life?

I can't, and I won't be able to assuage every apprehension you have, but I will tell you that your reluctance to rush and agree with me is welcome here. Together, we're going to make space for a few of the reasons that women just don't rest, a few of the lies that keep us from receiving this good gift. But we're also going to shine the light of the gospel on these untruths and see if we can't find a way forward.

Because no matter how skeptical we are, we can all agree: Jesus Christ did not die on the cross for us to live a life of punitive exhaustion. And if we're tired of being tired, imagine how much our gracious and merciful Father wants to see us break free from the fatigue cycles that keep us bound.

Let's dive in together. Here are five lies that you might believe about rest, and the truths that I believe just might set us free.

Lie #1: "I can't rest until the work is done."

The chore I love most is laundry. And here's why: It's something I can finish. A few times a week, the kids bring all their clothes downstairs, I put Netflix on my iPhone with my headphones on, watch some *Grey's Anatomy* or *West Wing*, wash everything, fold everything, and then call the kids back down to get all their laundry. It's completed. It's done. At least for the day.

A few years back, Nick and I were both going through a rough patch in our callings. We were constantly discouraged, exhausted,

34

and having a hard time connecting with passion or purpose. After talking to a few wise people, we were encouraged to find hobbies that we could finish because nothing in our work was ever technically "done."

Parenting is never finished; you can't check it off a list. Pastoring isn't a task you can complete; there are always more people to love or lead. It's almost impossible to take a break from being the leader of a business; you can't pause it or step away without extensive planning. And after a break, you often come back to an overwhelming amount of catch-up.

I think many of us are waiting until we're "done" or "finished" before we rest. But that moment is not coming until the end of our life.

We're convinced that the laundry has to be done, every text has to be answered, every kid nurtured, and every important email responded to. Before we rest, we need to have a grip on the next week, we need to plan the next thing, and we need to finish the dishes.

And this is where I'm incredibly grateful for the very first vision of rest as cast in Genesis. Let's go line by line back to the beginning and see if we can't have our minds changed about needing to earn our rest.

> In the beginning God created the heavens and the earth. Now the earth was formless and empty, darkness was over the surface of the deep, and the Spirit of God was hovering over the waters. And God said, "Let there be light," and there was light. God saw that the light was good, and he separated the light from the darkness. God called the light "day," and the darkness he called "night." And there was evening, and there was morning—the first day. (Gen. 1:1–5)

First, just for fun, we're zooming in on Holy Spirit. The wild wind of our triune Godhead was there at creation. We also, of course, see evidence of Jesus later, in verse 26, as Father God references making man in "our" image, but for now, let's pay close attention to God the Spirit, and His participation in creation.

Most translations use the word *hovering*, but the Hebrew word used in Genesis 1:2 to describe the active state of Holy Spirit is *rachaph*, which means "to relax, move gently, cherish, or grow soft."

In one of the most pivotal moments of the universe, when everything had to be completed and nothing had yet been "finished," we find Holy Spirit relaxing. But there's more.

Just after God creates day and night, literal light and darkness, He does something interesting. Right here, in the foundation of everything, He switches the order on us: He shifts from the day-night pattern to night and then day.

One of my sons had this really cute habit growing up of saying numbers backward from the traditional order. If I asked him how many chicken nuggets he wanted, he'd say, "Oh, five or four will do!" Or when asked what time he wanted to be picked up from a friend's house, he'd reply, "Two or one o'clock!" We found it so endearing and amusing.

But Father God's switch-up right here is actually life-changing for those of us who feel we need to earn our rest. When our intentional and creative God speaks day and night into being, the original sequence is day and then night. But then it's like He pulls out the Uno Reverse card and suddenly begins referring to the two as evening and then morning. When it's time to put creation into play, for humans to inhabit it, night comes first. Rest comes first. And then work.

Right here, at the very beginning, we see God easing our fears and concerns about whether we'll ever be able to earn our rest. There is no list to finish before we take the gift that's offered to us from a good and loving Father. There is evening and morning, there is rest and then work. In God's structuring of the created order of everything, He intentionally sequenced rest to come *first* before any kind of waking activity. We break ties with the lie that we have to rest after our work is completed, and we receive the truth that we won't really be able to work well until we take the rest.

Every time I've experienced a significant change in my life, it's come like this: My mind has been changed, I've acted differently, and then I've felt differently.

Just because I told you (or reminded you) that there was evening and then morning, you won't immediately *feel* like you don't have to earn your rest. But what you can do is take this knowledge, begin to think differently about rest, start to act differently based on this knowledge, and then eventually you will feel like you don't need to earn rest.

Good news, right?

Lie #2: "Rest will be boring."

Have you noticed how it has become kind of "cool" in the past few years to have disdain for people? I kind of blame the internet and the overgeneralization of what it means to be an introvert. A few years ago, I noticed a lot of little memes online and jokes made at parties about how certain people hate people.

My husband noticed it too, and during a recent sermon, he made a joke that was so funny and convicting that the entire audience didn't know what to do when he said it.

Nick said, "Everyone is always joking about how they hate people now. It's too people-y outside. You love church, but it's the people that bother you. I'm here to remind you if you hate people, you're going to hate heaven."

The air felt still and electric until everyone eventually started laughing. But it's true, right? If we hate people, we should probably stop pretending that heaven is going to be a solo spa retreat. Instead, it's described as a great banquet, a wedding party, with too many people to count, all of us worshiping God.

I'm not trying to juke you, but let's go ahead and put this right here: If you hate rest, you're going to hate heaven.

Stick with me; don't close the book because I actually don't think you hate to rest. I'm willing to bet that one of a few things could possibly be true:

- *You resist rest because you assume it's not enjoyable.* You've tried to rest in the way you "should," and it's not been right for *you*, so instead of enjoying it so much that you look forward to it again, you avoid it altogether. My husband rests by sitting still. I genuinely hate sitting still. So one way I rest is by running. It recreates me; it helps me fight fatigue and striving. It helps me reconnect with God. It doesn't look like rest to others, but it absolutely is for me. We'll talk more about this later in the book.

- *You resist rest because you perceive it as being lazy or passive.* I think noticing this about ourselves is 90 percent of the battle. Once we put this thought pattern on the table in front of us and maybe spend a few minutes paying attention to where it came from (parents, a boss, a character on TV), we can speak the truth about it and move forward. If God our Father rested during creation, if Holy Spirit rested over the earth, if Jesus Christ Himself needed sleep and time away with God—rest cannot be lazy or sinful. And we can't continue living in this thought pattern. Amen?

- *You resist rest because you've grown more accustomed to striving for your worth than receiving it from God.* I'm sorry to speak so bluntly, but this is a lot of us, right? We hate rest because we've become so used to earning our love, our place, and our value with our work. And those momentary flashes of worldly glory are what our souls have become used to. The bad news is that they lose their fulfillment over time and leave us pushing harder and faster to be seen and valued. The good news is that, as I mentioned earlier, when we change our minds and then change our behavior, we often feel differently. You won't always crave the broken cycle of striving—if things begin to shift now.

You're not going to hate heaven.

If by grace through faith you have a relationship with Jesus, you're going to *love* heaven. We all are. We're not going to be disappointed or bored, and I don't believe we'll long to have a second of the fallen world back.

And there's even more fun news: We see evidence in Scripture that in eternity, there will also be cultivation. Before the fall in Genesis, there is cultivation. God calls Adam to *abad*. The Hebrew word means "to cultivate, or to serve." This means that before everything goes south, humans are given purpose and calling. The word used after the fall of humankind, the punishment for sin, is *toil*. That Hebrew word is *itstsabon*—which means "a pain."

There are also multiple references to work and cultivation (not toil) in eternity in both the Old and New Testaments. We're not going to lie on clouds and nap all day. There will be worship and relationship and cultivation in the form of meaningful action— just like in the garden of Eden before the fall. But there will also be rest—that's a promise from God, not a threat.

So, what if we learn to practice now for heaven? What if we have our minds changed, shift our patterns, and then start to feel like we love *not* being so tired all the time?

Lie #3: "No one else around me will rest."

Maybe you've read the books and tried to shift, but your partner or friends or boss hasn't exactly championed your desire for change. Maybe you've settled for a life of constantly being tired because you know that the community around you will never change its pace.

Perhaps the fear is that if you rest, you'll be seen as lazy. Or maybe you have grown to love being the dependable, busy, and exhausted one—you wear it as a badge of honor, and you're not sure who you are without it.

Wherever you find yourself, the truth remains: Most of our cultures promote and encourage a pace that leaves us near the end of our rope. Rarely will we find communities that are set up to embrace a collective kingdom-guided pace of life, and many of us will need to prepare for being misunderstood when we finally receive the gift of rest in our lives.

My favorite emoji is the two little hands pressed together, the palms facing upward. Technically it's called "palms up," but I send it to friends to signify, "I'm holding this with you." Whether it's grief, joy, or just a tension that can't be easily solved, I want to show that I'm in it with them.

I'm holding this with you.

I don't want to give you quick and pithy answers that make this seem like it will be easy. I could say, "You're not going to be worshiping your boss / mother / best friend / husband in heaven, so stop trying to please them with this pace of life that's killing you," but we both know it's more complicated than that.

For many of us, if we walk into our jobs tomorrow and say we're cutting back on our hours to fight the existential, deep, and spiritual exhaustion that we feel, we're not going to be met with encouragement or a raise.

For many of us, our fears are founded in historical evidence that slowing down or saying no will disappoint or even anger others.

For many of us, embracing a life of rest will actually make us the most countercultural person we know, even though we find ourselves in Christian circles and churches.

For many of us, making real and lasting shifts toward a more sustainable pace of life will only highlight just how different we are from everyone around us.

I'm holding this with you.

God has given us the gift we need to experience peace, health, and restoration in our souls. More than just giving us the gift of rest, He's also asked us to be obedient. I'm assuming this double whammy of invitation and commandment means that He knew it would be tough for us to obey.

Here's one more reason I don't think that the reaction and responses of other people should keep us from changing our lives: This is how the world changes.

One woman in a friend group begins to feel uncomfortable with gossip and begins lovingly changing the conversation. Soon after, the entire culture changes and all the women are speaking life and keeping each other's names safe.

One family in a church decides to foster or adopt, and what once seemed insurmountable or scary suddenly becomes an accessible way to obey God and serve His kids. Before much time passes, there is a culture of caring for orphans.

One community member begins to go against the grain and stand for what is good and whole. One person stands out and stands firm for something that matters, and others take note. What if you're the catalyst for kingdom change? What if your being tired of being tired is the impetus for an entire cultural shift?

Later in this book, we'll talk about how we can practically communicate our boundaries for rest and invite others into rhythms that bring them peace and restoration. For now, let's hit a couple more major concerns you might have.

Lie # 4: "It's going to cost too much."

As I was dreaming about this book, preplanning where I wanted to go and how you and I would genuinely fight the fatigue that's trying to take us out, I thought I wanted to call it *Risky Rest*. Just before I started writing, I realized that wasn't the best title, but I wanted to be honest and up-front right from the get-go about what this is going to cost us.

If you're tired of being tired, embracing kingdom rest will not be a risk-averse path. I believe it will require something from us more times than not.

Here's where I will level with you: Choosing rest will cost you. But here is the excellent news: The cost is really just a trade, making space for us to receive a far greater gift than anything we might be giving up.

Rest may cost us the approval of others, but it will help us gain a sense of being known and loved by God.

Rest may cost us the rewards of worldly striving, but it will help us experience eternal abundance.

Rest will cost us the identity of being "the most counted on" but will give us wild peace and contentment.

Rest will cost us a life pushed to its limits but will bless us with one that embraces boundaries.

Maybe if you embrace rest, you will risk the way your relationships have always been. Maybe others will judge you, praise you less, or even break communion with you. Or maybe . . . the people in your life will see the fruit of peace and be encouraged to follow suit. Maybe you'll lovingly show them the way so they can break free from the fatigue that's killing them too.

Maybe they'll find Jesus to be a kind and compassionate Friend rather than a drill sergeant demanding more of them by the day. Maybe they'll encounter a Father who gives rest to those He loves rather than asking them to earn it. Maybe they'll sense the nearness of a Spirit that rests on them as they embrace a life of risky rest.

Maybe you'll make less money this year, or your kids will be involved in fewer activities. Maybe your life won't look like you pictured or assumed it was supposed to go. Or maybe . . . you'll find a life with more depth than the cultural norms that are expected of you. Maybe you'll be able to savor and enjoy your life because you're present and rested for it.

Maybe you'll have to give up the perception of yourself that you were told was essential to uphold. Maybe you won't be the most dependable, but you'll find dependence on God. Maybe you won't be the one people call in the middle of the night, but they'll call on Him instead. Maybe others will be able to make assumptions about you and be free to misunderstand you, but you'll be free not to carry the weight of that pursuit.

Maybe you won't live the distracted, breakneck speed that you're used to, but instead you'll learn what it means when Jesus says He wants to show you an easy yoke and a light burden.

Maybe this is going to change everything.

Maybe that's great.

Lie #5: "My circumstances won't allow for it."

If you're already thinking, *This girl doesn't get it*, I can save you some energy by confirming, I do not, in fact, understand every circumstance in your life that makes you feel so tired. I don't know what it's like in your world, the demands that are asked of you, the people you have to take care of. I don't know your budget.

And thankfully, the purpose of this book is not to provide a cookie-cutter proclamation of what rest should look like for every woman. Rather, here's what I'm praying happens as you read the chapters ahead:

I'm praying you really do get tired of being tired—if you weren't already. I'm praying you feel enough grief over the state of exhaustion you've been in that you're willing to trust God one more time as you attempt rest.

I'm praying that as you hear stories of biblical truth, your life begins to transform as your mind begins to be renewed by kingdom truth. I know that our lives are often changed when our minds are changed first, and I pray that happens as you allow yourself to read these stories and principles.

I pray that you encounter practical tips for realistic rest. I promise not to suggest you quit everything and go on a silent retreat if you promise to try at least a few of the Low Power Mode ideas or practical suggestions.

Finally, I pray you catch a vision of embracing rhythms of rest in every season of your life so you can draw near to God over and over again as your life throws new levels of tired at you.

I don't get your whole life. I don't see every facet of what is difficult about it. I don't know every circumstance, so I cannot remove every catalyst of exhaustion in your life. But I am moved by compassion to sit with you, at least figuratively, as we ask God how in the world we can learn the rested life from Him. I cannot answer every circumstance, but I believe with all that I've got—our Father can bring some form of rest in every season. And I will stand firm in faith for you, even if you're scared or skeptical.

This book is for you.

I trust God to meet you here because that's what He does when His daughters seek Him.

Low Power Mode

Because giving you a long list of things to do would be exhausting and not helpful, you only have one action item for Low Power Mode in this chapter. Take it as an invitation, not an obligation:

Maybe for the time it takes you to read this book, ask God to help you put the rest of your skepticism down. To be honest, it takes a lot of energy to critique a process while you're in it. So, what if, for however long you're reading, you commit to not spending your precious energy on doubting whether you'll ever stop feeling tired.

four

find the fatigue

When one of my kiddos was being born, one of their older siblings was having a hard time adjusting. I'm not sharing which kid was being born and which one was having a hard time on the off chance that my kids will read this one day—no shame, Connolly kids, amen?

My son (the older sibling) went from cuddly and connected to withdrawn and distant almost overnight when the younger one was born. It seemed natural and then got more extreme and discouraging as time passed. My older child would cry when the baby was close to him and didn't want to be near me anymore.

With the birth of the new baby, I'd had a pretty traumatic C-section. My health had been tenuous before the delivery and was very tender afterward. I didn't think our kids had noticed it too much, but I wondered if this was playing into my son's reaction, and I asked another mom friend for advice.

She suggested I ask my older child if he felt hurt by all my body had been through because of this baby, and she encouraged me to ask it in some interesting ways. "He may not be able to express it in feelings yet, so ask if it hurts his body." This sounded pretty out there to me, but I was willing to do anything to help my kid express what was burdening him.

One night when everyone else was settled and distracted, I sidled up as close to him as possible and asked, "Does it hurt you that Mommy had a new baby?" He shook his head no.

As soon as he started crying, I couldn't get much more out of him. So I patted his back, wiped his tears, and told him I was OK and, of course, that it wasn't this new baby's fault that I had been in pain. But then I tried the body question just out of curiosity. "Does it hurt your body anywhere that Mommy got hurt?" He started sobbing again and nodded. "Yes—it hurts my back."

I found this so incredibly fascinating, and I was so grateful for the wisdom of my friend. My son let me rub his back and comfort him, and I was intentional over the next few weeks to let him see me recovering and to affirm that this new baby was no threat to our health. But I'll never forget how stunned I was to see emotional pain manifesting as physical pain in my young child. Of course, I knew this phenomenon was natural, but seeing this lived out in someone so young and how it helped him find his words and heal was unforgettable.

The pain of your fatigue, the saturation point where it manifests itself as tension in your life, is telling a bigger truth and is something we need to pay attention to and address. We need to ask individually, "Where does it hurt? Where are you tired to tears? Where has the exhaustion become unbearable?" But for us to experience lasting healing from the fatigue we've been carrying our whole lives, we'll also have to dive deeper into the source of the pain, knowing that the source of the injury may not be the same as the site of the irritation.

To stop living tired, we have to know where we're tired and why. Here are some examples.

· · · · · · · · · · ·

Tiffany is a woman on a mission. Since she met Jesus in her late teens, she's been fueled with passion and purpose. She listens to God and obeys Him and loves reading the Word and serving others. She's a mom of two young kids and wants to do everything she can to raise them with faith, compassion, and kindness. Unfortunately, the last few years have been tenuous for her family as she's experienced resurfacing trauma from her past combined with present-day stress.

Everything would be doable if she could get a full night's sleep, but her four-year-old still doesn't sleep that great and climbs into her bed most nights. She is so tired, and the main pain point for her seems to be physical exhaustion. However, spiritual fatigue has set in from decades of wanting to please God and not understanding how valuable she is to Him before she even does a thing. On top of that, she's got emotional fatigue from making space for everyone else's feelings and never taking time to experience and process her own.

She needs more sleep, yes. But she also is desperate for someone to remind her about what the gospel actually means for her. She could really use help fighting the fear that creeps in when she's trying to fall asleep. And if she took the time to care for her own emotions, she might not feel like she's always holding her breath and avoiding being alone.

. . . .

Nicole is in her early twenties and, by all appearances, should be living her best life. She got a job she loves right out of college (she was the first in her family to go), she's obsessed with her friends and church community, she journals regularly to keep her heart and mind in a good spot, and she just started going to therapy once a month to do maintenance check-ins.

But every so often a breakdown builds, and she can't catch her breath. It starts with a few days of feeling off, then the tears come out of nowhere, and when the fatigue sets in, she cancels everything she can for about forty-eight hours and stays in bed. She swears she's not depressed, and she doesn't think it's linked to her menstrual cycle—but she's tried so hard to figure out what's wrong with her and feels so much shame about the roller coaster she keeps going on.

The truth is, her schedule is just too full, and her "best life" is now just a tick too busy for her body to maintain. She's learned to push down the symptoms of physical exhaustion daily because life feels so great, and she has difficulty saying no. Her fear of missing out and her deep desire to live an abundant life keep her in a state of almost constant burnout, but she can't see it because the "stress" isn't harmful—it's all life-giving and enjoyable.

. . . .

Jackie is an even-keeled, single mom of three teens who works from home in human resources. All of her friends say they feel the same way she does, a little scattered and constantly behind, so she's learned not to worry too much about the frazzled feeling she walks around with. She can never seem to remember what the sermon at church was about halfway through the week, and while that makes her feel shame, she's not sure there's anything she can do about it.

She wonders if life is all lists and unfinished tasks for everyone else. She wonders where Jesus is in the midst of her messy-middle life. She's tired but mostly just tired of not being fully awake to what's happening around her. But before she can dig into that problem, she's on to the next thing. She would pray about it, but she forgets. Her time with God in the morning is often interrupted by a quick scroll on social media, and her nighttime routine is full of taking care of everyone else until she watches the show that she's slowly making her way through—that's how she shuts her brain off every night.

Her mental exhaustion is just a way of life, right? She knows she used to be a deep thinker; she used to have margin, and she hopes one day she'll get it back.

. . . .

Natalie is an empty nester who lives what outwardly seems to be a restful life. She works part-time at her friend's shop, not for financial gain but because it's exciting to see the new clothes come in and catch up with the shoppers. Her only grandchild lives a few states over, and she travels to visit him as often as her daughter-in-law will allow. Her husband swears he will retire soon, but to be honest, she loves that she has a season of free time while he's still pretty occupied.

She's in a blissful season of sleep, getting eight or nine hours most nights, leisurely waking up with tea and her Bible, and then enjoying multiple stretches of quiet before she falls asleep every night. So, why in the world is she so tired?

She grew up in a time when it was not only impolite to process your emotions, it was selfish and dramatic. Also, what in the world does she have to complain about? Her life is great, so she zips up her feelings and hasn't let her deep emotions hit the surface for years. But the trauma of her past sneaks up out of nowhere; she'll watch a sad movie and feel exhausted for days after. When she goes to a Christian women's conference, she goes in feeling exuberant and leaves feeling fatigued from the pressure of pushing down what lies just beneath the surface.

For someone who isn't that outwardly emotional, the energy it takes to just make it through the day without bursting into tears is sometimes out of this world. No amount of naps, vacations, or quiet time seems to help her feel rested. She can't figure out why she is still so tired.

Types of Exhaustion

A one-size-fits-all plan to rest will not work for us because we're all tired in incredibly different ways. And while our exhaustion may be expressed in one area, we may be experiencing the most fatigue in another.

This is why many of us still feel tired after a vacation, grumpy after a nap, listless when we take a day off, or completely drained when we leave events that were supposed to be refreshing.

Throughout this book, we're going to walk through the individual areas of fatigue to find where we struggle the most, but first, you and I must understand how each kind of tiredness is different. Once we find the source of our fatigue, we can rest in the ways our souls currently require.

Spiritually Tired

With the arrival of Jesus, the Messiah, that fateful dilemma is resolved. Those who enter Christ's being-here-for-us no longer have to live under a continuous, low-lying black cloud. A new power is in operation. The Spirit of life in Christ, like a strong wind, has magnificently cleared the air, freeing you from a fated lifetime of brutal tyranny at the hands of sin and death. (Rom. 8:1–2 MSG)

He interrupted me while I was sweeping.

I was in my midtwenties when my husband pulled me aside as I was aggressively cleaning the house, sat me down on our cheap,

49

brown faux-leather sofa, and tried to explain the gospel to me. I'd been a believer in Jesus for over ten years at the time. I'd even taught a few Bible studies and written a few articles on scriptural insights, but something tipped Nick off to a gnawing in my heart that needed to be addressed.

It didn't matter how gentle or humble he sounded; I couldn't help but bristle with pride when he asked if I understood the gospel. "Of course I know what the gospel is! It's the Good News!" I had heard that in a sermon somewhere.

"But that Good News is the answer to a problem. Do you know what the bad news is?" he replied.

I wanted a witty retort that showed him how knowledgeable I was, but the words weren't coming. And now that I was on the spot, there was a nagging fear in the back of my mind that maybe I didn't even understand what the Good News was.

I rushed some words out of my mouth about Jesus loving us, again my feelings hurt and my hackles raised. He affirmed what I knew to be true, that Jesus did love me and us, but he also said the Good News was an antidote to the bad news that left me feeling condemned and wanting.

The bad news was that I wasn't enough on my own. I couldn't try hard enough. My intentions were never totally just. My best would always fall flat. And the worst news was that I wouldn't have chosen Jesus and couldn't earn His love, even if I tried to do everything right.

The Good News was that He chose me first. The Good News was that He handed His righteousness to me as a gift, an identity that I could take and run with, and there was a safety and belonging I had access to before I ever tried to do something right but eventually messed up.

The Good News was that Jesus saved me once and for all at the wild moment of salvation, and He kept saving me and extending grace, forgiveness, and redemption as I ultimately needed it day after day.

The bad news was that I wasn't the best mom, the most faithful pastor's wife, the kindest friend, the most secure minister of the gospel, or even the godliest wife.

The Good News was that I was loved no matter what, and God had placed me where I was on purpose for His glory and the good of others, to be His ambassador and daughter just as I was—no pretending or striving needed.

Why did my husband interrupt my aggressive sweeping session to give me this gospel pep talk? Because I had been pushing that broom back and forth, blinking back frustrated tears about my lack of capacity to have it all together. He saw my breakdown for the tenth time that week as I balked and crumbled at my humanness. And somehow, because he sees me and loves me for exactly who I am, he knew this was not a physical or emotional exhaustion—this was spiritual.

I'd forgotten the gospel, and it had left me so entirely tired of being me. A misunderstanding of the gospel and grace will leave us exhausted in our soul, our bones, at the very core of our being.

Spiritual exhaustion manifests itself in many ways:

You may be weary from trying to earn your place in the kingdom.

You may be tired from spiritual abuse, manipulation, or spaces that call for striving.

There may be a lack of peace and stillness in your life because you've lost your appreciation for the mystery or awe of eternal things, and you're determined to understand every precept.

Spiritual exhaustion may have set in if you're living in a have-to versus a get-to mentality about spiritual rhythms.

You may also be spiritually tired if you've stopped seeing and seeking abundance and have instead begun only to operate out of obligation.

What's interesting about my sweeping situation is that anyone else would have looked at my life in that season and assumed I was physically exhausted. I had three kids under three at the time and got very little sleep. My life was also incredibly isolated, as I lived three thousand miles from family and shared a car and cell phone with my husband, so some might have assumed I was emotionally tired. I'm not sure anyone would have thought I was mentally fatigued because the most pressing question in my day was often whether we should watch *Dinosaur Train* before or after nap time, but you get my point.

After that conversation, I could see a clear delineation in my spirit, ministry, joy, and overall mental health. Once I noticed the spiritual striving and fatigue that had set in, I got counseling and began having honest conversations about the gospel and grace. I memorized Romans 8:1, "There is therefore now no condemnation for those who are in Christ Jesus" (ESV), and splattered my house with sticky notes that reminded me of God's mercy and kindness.

Spiritual exhaustion will seep into our marrow. It will languish in our bones and hollow our spirits. It can often be hard to determine that our fatigue is spiritual, and it will take courage to admit that our souls are where we need the relief. But once we get the help we need, it will feel like someone turned on the lights just when we couldn't stand the dark any longer.

Physically Tired

> It's useless to rise early and go to bed late,
>> and work your worried fingers to the bone.
> Don't you know he enjoys
>> giving rest to those he loves? (Ps. 127:2 MSG)

Fun spoiler alert: Even though we just covered spiritual fatigue, every version of exhaustion is often based on spiritual mistruth, and our recovery in each area has eternity-sized implications. Your physical body doesn't live in a vacuum away from your soul. Rather, all our types of tired are interconnected, like the veins, fascia, neurons, and nerves in our body.

That being said, sister—some of us just need a nap.

You know who you are. You don't need a long essay from me, do you?

We've convinced ourselves that five hours of sleep is OK for us. We're built differently. We don't need a day off from exercise. We'd hate to know what that would mean about us. No, we don't mind moving the meeting up a half hour earlier, even though that means we'll be up two hours later tonight prepping the notes. We've grown so used to pushing our bodies past their intended limits, we get an endorphin high from feeling a little sore or tired—we falsely believe that means we're doing it right.

I have promised not to shame my sisters in Christ in this book, so I want you to picture me in your midst with a sheepish look. I have worn my exhaustion like a badge of honor. I have judged my friends who get more than seven hours of sleep, and I have set the alarm earlier and earlier to meet more and more expectations.

And I have seen, as I mentioned in the previous chapter, that there are no winners in the competition to see who can live the least rested. If we continue to say that we'll sleep when we're dead, we may get our wish sooner rather than later. Not only will our physical bodies fail us if we ignore their needs, warnings, and desperate cries for help, but worse, we will live half awake if we don't get enough sleep.

I fell asleep on the way to my wedding rehearsal and will never forget it. My mom and stepdad were up front, my big sister was in the back seat with me, I was wearing the supercute tea-length white dress I'd picked out weeks before, and on the fifteen-minute drive to the church, I just conked out. I remember snapping back to wakefulness and thinking, *This is messed up! If I'm tired enough to fall asleep, my veins coursing with Diet Coke and bride energy, my body seriously needs sleep.*

The question is, Will we be brave enough to ask why we settle for physical exhaustion? What will we find when we ask how we got here, why we refuse to rest, and what we're scared of happening when we do?

Physical exhaustion is a little easier to spot than other types, but look for these warning signs in your life:

You might have grown accustomed to physical exhaustion if you often humblebrag about how little sleep you got last night.

You might be physically exhausted if you can make it through the day without napping but often lose focus or forget to be present.

Physical exhaustion may be the main problem for you if you insist on arriving five minutes early or staying after everyone is gone.

You may need to address your physical exhaustion if you find pride in denying your body its basic needs to prove that you can.

You might be at a critical level of physical fatigue if your body gives you warning signals like anxiety, sleeplessness, chronic diseases, or adrenal fatigue.

For many of us, pride is the root issue associated with being physically tired. We have negative connotations with rest that lead us to thoughts of laziness, indulgence, and lack of trustworthiness.

Together we'll gently uproot the lies around rest and our bodies and look to the life of Jesus to find physical rest in this good land we inhabit. It's going to be good, I promise.

Mentally Tired

I'm telling you these things while I'm still living with you. The Friend, the Holy Spirit whom the Father will send at my request, will make everything plain to you. He will remind you of all the things I have told you. I'm leaving you well and whole. That's my parting gift to you. Peace. I don't leave you the way you're used to being left—feeling abandoned, bereft. So don't be upset. Don't be distraught. (John 14:25–27 MSG)

Before I pry my eyes open, the list starts. First, I remember the things from yesterday that didn't get finished. The shame swirls in my mind as I pull the covers further up to my face. I sort out those past-due to-dos without opening my eyes but starting to stretch my toes and wake up my legs.

I reach under the cool side of the pillow, grab my phone, and turn off the alarm that never even got to go off as I slip on my robe and sneak quietly out of the bedroom. I walk into the kitchen to turn on the coffee maker, and the leftover list of things undone is blinking bright red in my mind as I pick a mug and hit Brew. It's time to make an actual list, so I open the Notes app on my phone before I forget what I've just now remembered.

When I open the Notes app, I'm discouraged to find the list I started a few days ago and never finished. I add to it, open Instagram while I wait for the coffee to finish, and scroll mindlessly until I see my former friend turned extreme conspiracy theorist. I can't decide what's scarier: this new inflammatory piece of fake news she's just posted or the idea of talking to her about it. I close the app, grab the mug, pick up my Bible, and pad my way to the sofa for a few minutes of quiet time before the rest of the house wakes up.

I open my Bible study to where I last left off, and I'm honestly annoyed with myself that I don't even remember this passage I was studying. How can I ever grow in my faith if I don't recall what I meditate on each morning as I'm living my life? I switch between studying, journaling, jotting down little notes and prayers, and reopening the Notes app to add to my incomplete list of important tasks.

I hear someone else's alarm go off in the house. The fatigue leaves my limbs heavy and my soul weary already. How am I tired before the day has even started?

Mental fatigue is not the exception. It's the culturally insistent rule. For most of us, it is assumed that we will be bombarded with information from the moment we open our eyes until we close them at night. There is a worldwide assumption that you will adhere to a policy of being accessible at all times via your phone. There's an implied insistence that we, as women, will do the mental gymnastics needed to cope with and coordinate the complicated lives of every person we lead and love.

If you're mentally tired, it makes sense. And if you need rest in your thoughts, spirit, and strategic processing, you will have to be OK with swimming against the cultural stream.

Look for these warning signs that you're struggling with mental exhaustion:

You might be mentally tired if you're increasingly struggling to remember days, names, or details.

You might struggle with mental fatigue if your thoughts are obsessive, intrusive, or overly anxious.

You might need mental rest if you constantly seek distraction to escape the overwhelming thoughts, plans, and problems you can't quite sort out.

Mental exhaustion might have set in if you've lost your creative spark, joy, or passion for using your God-given gifts.

You may be tired mentally if you always wish you had a little more time to plan, process, or perfect what you want to say or do.

You might struggle with mental fatigue if you wrestle with making wise decisions on time or feel frightened when presented with multiple opportunities.

Mental fatigue does not have to be our norm. God has given us the person of Jesus, our Prince of Peace. He's given us sound minds and strategies to sort out the constant barrage of thoughts, plans, and problems. Our anxiety and other mental struggles are not signs that our brains are broken but rather proof that we live under the effects of a fallen world.

If feeling distracted, confused, and like you're falling behind has become your normal, mental rest will change your life.

Emotionally Tired

We feel needless shame about our fatigue, and Lord knows we feel shame about our tears. And yet, we see that crying, specifically due to emotional fatigue, is incredibly biblical.

> My tears have been my food
> day and night,
> while people say to me all day long,
> "Where is your God?"

56

> These things I remember
>   as I pour out my soul:
> how I used to go to the house of God
>   under the protection of the Mighty One
> with shouts of joy and praise
>   among the festive throng. (Ps. 42:3–4)

"I don't know why I'm crying," she says.

My friend sits across from me, trying to quickly tick the tears off her cheeks, looking like she wishes she could will them back where they came from. She doesn't know why she's crying, but goodness gracious, I sure do.

Maybe it's the trauma of her past that everyone told her she had no right to process. Maybe it's that her life seems overwhelming—loving and leading and serving and showing up constantly for everyone else. Maybe we just made it through the holidays, and the tiny paper cuts of relationship pain from a family that doesn't process trauma are freshly stinging every single nook and cranny of her soul. Maybe it's the world that seems to be crashing down around us culturally—and every news report is a damning reminder of what we're up against.

She doesn't know why she's crying as she tells me about this tough conversation with another friend, but I don't know how she's kept the tears at bay this long.

I've learned this about feelings: If we don't make space for our emotions and pay full attention to what they're telling us, they'll spill out onto every other area of our lives.

Our emotions are our telltale heart, just like Poe's crazy corpse's that kept beating louder than anyone could bear. Unprocessed emotions are like a boulder we carry while we run a marathon, and we can't figure out why we're so tired—even though we trained for this. We can't figure out why we're crying, but I sense that Holy Spirit hovers over us, desiring us to take the comfort we're offered.

Emotional fatigue is terrible at obeying boundaries and borders; rather, it seeps into every crevice it can find. The tears we fight contort our faces until we run out of the room to keep from being found out. Our capacity or lack of ability to be comforted by God, to feel in front of Him, and to receive what He offers is the connective tissue tying our emotions to our eternal state of being. And even when we long to be all business, to keep things tidy in our minds, our emotions break into our conscious and unconscious thoughts, filtering and shading every interaction and engagement.

Here are a few indicators you're struggling with emotional fatigue:

You might be emotionally tired if you can no longer access compassion for others.

You might be emotionally exhausted if your usual mode of operation is to stuff your feelings and vow to think about them later.

You might be experiencing emotional fatigue if you find yourself pretending to experience what everyone else is expressing—whether that's positive or negative.

Emotional exhaustion could be an issue for you if you find yourself expressing negative emotions toward people who don't deserve them.

You might be emotionally tired if you can't get past certain emotions and it feels like they're here to stay forever.

While I'm not a therapist (but goodness gracious, they've changed my life and helped me know God and myself better), I know our emotions are essential to our health. And I know that they can sap our energy like unseen cancers, taking what is vibrant and making it dull.

What if making more space for your emotions and processing them with God is the answer to what makes you so incredibly exhausted this season? And wouldn't that also make sense for those who are resting their faces off and never feeling renewed?

Where Are You Most Fatigued?

Finding the point of your fatigue is pivotal to breaking the cycle of exhaustion in your life. Chances are that as you've read through these descriptions, one or more of the types of exhaustion have stood out for you. But I also have a tool to help you check in with your current reality.

Below you'll find a short quiz to help you scan yourself and see where you're the most tired. You might find that you're fatigued in multiple areas, and that's incredibly common and good news. It means there's even more healing and hope ahead for you.

Be as honest as you can with yourself and God.

Let's throw off shame for where we're at and put on hope for where we're going.

1. When I'm tired, I usually know because . . .
   A. I feel critical of others and doubtful of God.
   B. my literal body aches—from my head to my toes.
   C. I can't think straight and can't finish a thought or a sentence easily.
   D. the tears pop up out of nowhere.

2. If I could fix one thing it would be . . .
   A. the soul-crushing weight of being human.
   B. my energy level would be enough for my life.
   C. I'd feel clear and ready for each day when it starts.
   D. I'd feel adequate and capable for my relationships.

3. I find myself wishing I was able to . . .
   A. feel connected to my soul.
   B. feel present in my body.
   C. feel clear in my thoughts.
   D. feel in control of my emotions.

4. The first thing I drop when I'm tired is . . .
   A. my capacity to pray and talk to God.
   B. the physical rhythms that keep me feeling healthy.
   C. making time and space to think or dream.
   D. processing my emotions and feelings.

5. I feel most relieved when . . .

   A. someone tells me they're praying for me and that they see me growing.

   B. plans get canceled.

   C. I make a wise decision or it's made for me.

   D. I realize I've made it through a tough situation without breaking down.

6. I wish someone else would . . .

   A. feed me spiritually.

   B. take physical burdens off my plate.

   C. handle the plans and details of my life.

   D. sit with me while I sort through what's going on in my life.

7. My dream retreat or vacation involves . . .

   A. getting some good teaching and soul care.

   B. naps, quiet, and lying by a pool.

   C. a good fiction book I can get lost in.

   D. a friend or therapist I can talk with for hours.

This quiz isn't the be-all and end-all to help you find where you're most fatigued. More than anything, I pray that reading the questions and answers shook loose some honest thoughts about what kind of tired you might be.

That being said, if you answered

- Mostly *A*s: Pay close attention to the portion of this book about spiritual exhaustion. Remember that it presents in many different ways, but there is so much hope ahead in these pages for you.
- Mostly *B*s: It may be that physical exhaustion is what plagues you the most in this season.
- Mostly *C*s: Mental exhaustion is real, and it permeates our lives. I'm praying that section of the book will serve you well.

- Mostly *D*s: You may be struggling with emotional exhaustion. Take stock as you read about how your feelings and emotions are showing up in other areas.

If your answers were all over the map, that sounds about right because our exhaustion in every sphere is interconnected. And there's great news for all of us: There is so much healing ahead.

In the coming chapters, you'll find a breakdown of each particular problem of fatigue and God's promise for us as we encounter it in our lives. I want to caution you to read not only the chapters pertaining to where you currently perceive that you're struggling. First of all, you may find solace and insight in areas you didn't even know were a problem for you. Second of all, as the seasons of your life shift, so do your areas of fatigue. I'd much rather you be armed and ready to fight any kind of tired that's coming for you and have information to serve those around you as well.

We're armed with the information of where we're most fatigued, or at least have a better sense of that than we had when we started. We're ready to face the problems that our push-through, busy-obsessed, and boundary-denying culture has caused in our lives. But we're also eager to plunge into the promises of God and come back with even more clarity about His character. Let's forge ahead bravely.

What Women Have to Say

I've lived most of my life without ever considering that there were four different types of tired. I think I've always just lumped them into two: physical or mental/emotional. But realizing that we can pull those apart and then address a spiritual tired as well has been so eye-opening. Knowing the cause of my fatigue is the first step in doing something about it.

Erin, wife, mom of teenagers, church staff member

five

spiritual exhaustion

"I just need to get through the next few weeks."

I love a good meme or hilarious quote that makes its way around the internet. Some of my favorites are the following:

> The real miracle Jesus performed was having twelve friends in his thirties.

> Sitting in your car outside your house is self-care. I don't know why—it just is.

> You don't go to Target because you need something. You go to Target and let Target tell you what you need.

I don't love when a meme starts making its way around the internet and settles in our hearts as truth but is actually a horrible lie that will mess with us for the rest of our lives.

And in that category, I'd like to present Exhibit A, my least favorite meme phrase:

> Adulthood is a cycle of constantly saying, "I just have to get through these few weeks," repeatedly.

Of course, I hate it because I've said it way too often myself. But probably right around the first time I saw a little graphic with this quote pop up, I began questioning if there was potentially any other way for me, for us, to live.

Because, friends, I can't do it anymore.

I refuse to keep living a life where the best I can hope for is an endless loop of exhaustion and listless living.

I refuse to live a life where I'm numb all day until I eventually crash, constantly hypnotized by hurry, and missing the million tiny miracles of every day.

Unfortunately, the depiction of spiritual exhaustion has become so normal—it's like one big inside joke we all make about ourselves. Spiritual exhaustion becomes our reality when we trade God's care for our obligation, God's grace for earning love, and God's abundance for just getting through the day.

And at the very core of my soul, I cannot believe that Jesus meant for us to live like this. I cannot imagine that our loving Father, who created us with care and creativity, who placed us on earth as an act of glorifying Himself, who sent His Son to redeem our souls, who gave us the Spirit that raised Jesus Himself from the dead . . . I cannot imagine He wants us to live at a pace that leaves us so exhausted that our only option is getting through.

Every single expression of exhaustion (physical, mental, and emotional) hinges on a spiritual tension that we as women of God have to explore: If God loves us and He gives rest to those He loves, then why are we living so incredibly tired and accepting this as our only possible reality?

Why are we buying the lie that our lives are not meant to be abundant, whole, and free but instead exhausted, overextended, and desperate for relief?

At its core, the fact that we're tired of being tired is a spiritual issue, and we need renewal in the form of spiritual revival as much as we need a nap, a day off, or a smaller to-do list.

As spiritual beings, we need spiritual solutions for our problems, including exhaustion. If we want to heal, we have to start here. Let's dive into the scriptural, spiritual, and eternal truths about our relationship with rest. Then let's ask God to renew our minds and help us find literal rest in our souls and let that same peace radiate throughout our lives.

Know Your Place

My kids are church kids through and through. All the stereotypes? They fit them.

They're somehow equal parts eager to serve and ready to bring chaos and mischief. We planted Bright City Church when they were seven, six, five, and one, and now our house is full of teenagers—so they've grown up with our church and are as comfortable there as they are at home. Too comfortable sometimes? Sure.

Do they sometimes steal the church kitchen snacks and start fires in the trash can during pre-service prayer? Yes. Do they simultaneously help lead kids' ministry when we can't get volunteers and keep the sound and slides rolling? Yes.

But we're a small church (in size—not heart!), so it's almost always all-hands-on-deck. And our family loves that this is our thing. We all love serving in our roles and bringing a little spice to what most people expect from the pastor's family.

While fighting my own fatigue, I stepped back a good bit from leading at Bright City last year, but sometimes people forget and still come to me for help. There's one church concern that was always my least favorite to handle, and I was so grateful to give it up for good: kids' behavior issues in Bright Kids.

It usually started with a post–Sunday service phone call letting me know there had been a problem and my intervention was needed. There's nothing worse than trying to casually tell a mom in a shame-free way that her kid bit another while also taking the whole thing seriously so you can keep other kids safe.

That being said, when I got a dreaded post-church text a few months ago letting me know there had been an issue in Bright Kids and asking if I could hop on the phone, I was thrilled to respond, *Oh, hey! I'm not sure if you heard. I'm actually not leading in this capacity anymore. You should call the kids' ministry director, and they'll help you sort this out!*

I put my phone down, relieved to be off the hook but curious about what had gone down that day.

My big kids had been serving or snoozing in the main service, so I turned to Cannon, our nine-year-old, to get some intel on what had gone down in Kids. Sure, he's nine, but he basically functions as a de facto pastor back there. He knows the kids with sensory processing needs and tries to help them. He loves to help the teacher get snacks and lead the student worship time. This is his turf, and he knows it.

Cannon looked at me with the world's most earnest, shocked face and said, "I can't think of any issues that happened in Bright Kids today. Everyone was behaving well."

It was right around then that my phone buzzed once more, and I saw the words, *Sorry—I should have been more clear. Cannon was the child we were having an issue with today. Can you hop on the phone real quick?*

The humbled and hilarious laugh that broke out of my mouth just then was filled with surprise and the reminder of something I'd always known: Cannon is as precocious as they come, which is compounded by the fact that he's also incredibly charming, so every time he does something a little sneaky, there's a temptation to laugh instead of discipline. Add to that the fact that we probably instill leadership values a little too heavily into our kids, and lo and behold, I had a kid who probably didn't understand his place, and this misunderstanding was causing him to take on more than he was ever meant to.

What followed was a grace-filled correction session, a conversation with all of our kids about respect and behavior, and a hearty reminder that they get to receive and be led at church. They're not soldiers, staff members, or even examples; they're kids. And while they shouldn't let anyone look down on them for their youth, they don't have to live like they're constantly on the hook. As the words poured out of my mouth and I thought about all the burdens I'd been carrying and the responsibilities that felt like rocks around my neck, I remembered the same was true for me too.

I also don't have to live like I'm constantly on the hook.

Like Cannon, I need constant reminders that I'm a child of God, not just a worker or a leader or a provider for other people in the kingdom.

And also, just like Cannon, I need to know my place, which will preserve me from taking on more than I am meant to.

Placed in Rest

The biblical theme of rest isn't the cherry on top of a message about trying hard to make God happy. It's not decorative or optional, something we can bypass or experience the fullness of God's kingdom without. The more we dig into Scripture, the more we'll see that He has embedded the invitation and gift of rest into the entire narrative of His people. This is wildly good news for you and me as we discover our true place and find that it's a place of rest.

Let's start in Genesis. We've already covered the references to our Triune God experiencing rest during creation and incarnation. But because we're studying our place, I want to look at what's happening with the humans in the garden of Eden. Go with me to Genesis 2:15: "The LORD God took the man and put him in the Garden of Eden to work it and take care of it."

OK, this doesn't sound very restful off the bat—until we dig into the Hebrew breakdown of language in this interesting verse. *Put* is the Hebrew word *yanach*, which means "to bestow, lay down, and rest." Whereas elsewhere, we most often see the Hebrew word *soom*, which simply means "to put or to place."

Putting these two thoughts together, we've been actively and intentionally placed in rest, and we've been called to cultivate. We see once again that work and rest are not at war. I pray this is good news for every single one of you who loves working and has felt shame because of that. There's nothing wrong with you if you love your work. Cultivation is a kingdom principle. When we work, we're giving God glory and living out who we were made to be in a beautiful way.

But in the beginning, when everything was right and as it should be, humankind was also placed into rest. Rest is not an optional add-on in God's kingdom; it's the place where we have always belonged. Because you and I are women who are renewed by the power of our minds, I want to underline this once more for all of us: Rest is not a result of the fall. Rest has always been a part of God's kingdom, and it is a gift God gives.

Rest isn't lazy or a sign that we're weak. Rest isn't a consolation prize for those who can't tough it out. Rest is where we're from, and it's also where we're going. The longer we misunderstand our eternal relationship with rest, the longer we won't know our place and the more exhausted we will become.

Practicing in Wilderness

If you're anything like me, reading about Adam and Eve can often feel very "other" and foreign, as if their reality doesn't apply to ours today. It's compelling and foundational to our faith, sure, but not crazy relatable since we don't walk with God in the cool of the morning or talk to snakes when we sin.

I know I can walk with God in the cool of the morning, but I live in Charleston, and we have about three cool mornings a year. I'm more of a "talk to God with my coffee and fuzzy robe when I climb back in bed" kind of gal, you know?

But the Israelites? The whiny, wonderful, brave, frightened, and often-found-wandering people of God—these guys I relate to. So,

I want us to look at how God placed the Israelites in rest to get a more realistic view of where God has also placed us today.

Here's a recap on God's chosen family, whom we follow through a lot of the Old Testament:

God made a promise to Abram (whom he later renamed Abraham) and his wife Sarai (later to become Sarah) that He would give them many sons, even though they couldn't have kids. Abraham ended up having a child with another woman out of doubt that the promise would come to fruition, but he and Sarah had one son, Isaac. Isaac had two sons, Esau and Jacob. After Jacob tricked Esau out of his birthright and wrestled with God, God changed his name to Israel, which means "has contended with God."

Israel had twelve sons who all moved to Egypt because of a famine. The twelve tribes (or larger family groups) grew exponentially until they became a threat to the Egyptians. At that point, the Egyptians enslaved them and terrible injustice ensued. At one point, the Egyptians became so threatened by the Israelites that their leader ordered all the baby boys to be put to death so that no more procreation or overpowering could happen. Moses was born during that time to an Israelite woman who hid him and put him in a basket in a river, hoping he'd float to safety.

He landed in the hands of the Egyptian king's daughter, grew up in the Egyptian palace, and later became overwhelmed and compelled by his people's pain. Moses then had a crazy encounter with God, who asked him to go back and help his people get free, and—after a little bickering—Moses said yes. Through a set of miracles, Moses got the people out of Egypt, and God started leading them to their place, a land He'd set aside especially for them.

The journey from Egypt to the promised land was supposed to take about ninety-two hours of walking, but instead, it took the Israelites forty years. Along the way they struggled with disobedience, complaining, anger, and idolatry. God kept showing up for them miraculously, even providing food and water in wild ways. He showed them signs, gave them guidelines, and proved His presence over and over again. But they constantly complained about their place. They wanted to go back to slavery or go ahead with the promise, but they continually missed the power of their present place.

Many theologians have proposed that the wilderness was the space God set aside for the Israelites to practice rest. Yes, there were struggles—they weren't at their place of destiny yet. There were hardships as well as sickness, sin, and fear about what would come next. But also, there were signs and miracles, and there was provision—everything they needed to build the muscles of rest for the promised land. And instead, they still struggled with striving, mistrust, and idol worship, which exhausted them.

As a reader, it's easy for me to look at the Israelites and get mad: "God is taking such good care of you! Why do you struggle so hard? Just chill and enjoy Him taking care of you!" But as a child of God, a daughter who often fights hard against the space I've been placed in, I also feel this tension. Don't you? Sometimes we can't quite zoom out and see where we're at, where we're supposed to be, or what we're supposed to be doing.

And so, we work, strive, push, say yes, stay up late, get up early, show up, serve, and try hard to be the hero in our stories and everyone else's. And then we burn out, numb, binge-watch TV, say a thousand nos, isolate, and then confuse rest with hiding from our lives until we course-correct and start working again.

We need to know our place.

To know our place in this now-and-not-yet season of our lives is to accept the invitation from our Father to believe that He wants abundance for us and not just reactive defeat. Reactive defeat says, it's always going to be this way; buckle up and get used to being tired.

Knowing our place empowers us to break ties with busy, no longer finding glory in filling our days just to fit in with everyone else.

Knowing our place, here on earth, will look like acknowledging our limitations and boundaries so that we can cultivate a sustainable pace rather than running forward at breakneck speed.

We need to know our place, and we need to know where we're going.

There's a Future Place

There's an elephant in the room when we talk about rest, and it's not a cute elephant. This is no Dumbo. This elephant is more like a hangry woolly mammoth with menstrual cramps, an animal of nightmare proportions that we'd rather ignore. It's the elephant you don't want to think about alone in the dark. So instead, we'll go together, flipping on the light of God's love and grace as we talk.

The elephant is this: The Bible clearly draws a correlation between death and rest.

When he's longing for death, Job says, "There the wicked cease from troubling, and there the weary are at rest" (Job 3:17 ESV).

Revelation 14:13 says,

Then I heard a voice from heaven say, "Write this: Blessed are the dead who die in the Lord from now on."

"Yes," says the Spirit, "they will rest from their labor, for their deeds will follow them."

When we bury someone, we say we're laying them to rest.

I'll never forget one of the most devastating texts I got from a friend who'd just lost her son. She was holding him in the hospital, saying goodbye, and she sent me a text saying, *I'm here holding him. He's sleeping.*

Death and rest are intertwined, for certain, but as you and I experience exhaustion here on earth, the problems of the living plague us. As we manage obligations, expectations, and overstimulated lives, the moment where our bodies cease all breathing feels a million miles away.

This past year, Nick and I did the whole detailed death-lawyer-will meeting that we'd put off for years. I thought it might feel morbid deciding who would get our kids and who'd be in charge of pulling the plug for us, but instead it was like looking the ugly woolly mammoth in the face without fear. Shortly after, I told Nick that I'd start to look into recording a sermon for my own memorial service or funeral each year on my birthday, just in case. He hated that idea, so I bartered and asked if I could film the opening and close.

I wasn't trying to be silly, and maybe I have an issue with always wanting the last word. But more than anything, I thought it might be helpful to open my eyes wide to the inevitability that I will leave this world one day. I imagined that starting each year of my life under the reality of my death would help me to live as if it mattered.

Here's a hypothesis of my own: What if our fear of death leads to our avoidance of the topic, and that's part of what's leading to our spiritual exhaustion? I see us doing this in a few ways.

When we ignore death, we try to make earth into heaven.

I once had a friend who wasn't sure she believed in heaven. I can be friends with almost anyone who believes almost anything. I'm more interested in figuring out how you got there and if you're willing, like I am, to keep learning.

But this particular lack of belief broke my heart because it just sounded like a devastating existence. Earth is hard, man. Life is defeating. And fleeting. And if there's nothing after this, I would be discouraged trying to find pure bliss, beauty, and perfection in this imperfect world.

If we're not in a regular rhythm of remembering the eternal truth that paradise is promised for those who walk with Jesus, the way we see the world gets wonky. We believe all the weight is on us to make this place as magical and amazing as possible. We end up believing this is all we get. And then, after all that striving, we see that it's just not as glittery as we imagined.

This is exactly how I felt the first time I went to Disney World as an adult. Supposedly, I went once as a kid, but I don't remember it. By the time I went back I was twenty-eight, and my kids accompanied me and my mom, stepdad, and little sister, Caroline. My mom, stepdad, and little sister are Disney people, and they'd been pumping me up about how I'd feel when we walked through the gates and saw the big castle . . . but that's not how it worked for me.

I was scared to let them see my face as I looked around, thinking, *Is this it?* Please don't send me emails if you're a Disney person. I'm not coming for your favorite place or pastime. I'm just saying it doesn't look like a beautiful castle to me. It looks like a small, fake castle. And also, there were 3,390 people in front of it taking selfies, and the Florida sun is scalding, making the experience even less majestic.

When we forget about death, we forget about heaven and exhaust ourselves trying to make the Disney castle of our lives seem like Buckingham Palace. It's not. Earth is not paradise, but our eternal home will be. And anticipating the rest and peace that we'll receive there and practicing for it now changes the game for us.

When we ignore death, we forget about the gospel.

Forgetting death distorts our experience of earth, causing us to settle for fake castles instead of the heavenly home Jesus is preparing for us. But forgetting death also distorts our understanding of purpose here on earth.

I'm obsessed with figuring out what people who don't believe in Jesus think about the afterlife. If it weren't rude, I'd want to grill every friend I have with the following questions:

- What do you think happens after we die?
- If there is a "good place," how will you know you're headed there?

The NBC show *The Good Place* covered these questions and themes, and if you can handle some light cursing in your TV viewing, I highly recommend watching it. If nothing else, it's research for helping to answer the existential questions of the people around us.

But honestly, this is a question that I think those of us who profess Jesus as our Savior could stand to answer every once in a while: How do you know you're headed to the good place? How does that happen?

The reason we need the refresher is simple: We forget. When we forget about death, we forget about heaven, and when we forget how we get to heaven, we forget the gospel. And when we forget the gospel, we live under the exhausting weight of the lie that we have to be good enough to have good things happen to us. When we forget the gospel, we'll strive and spin until we're so tired we can't stand. When we forget the gospel, we'll forget our purpose and begin acting as if God's love is something we can earn.

When we ignore death, we miss glimpses of the eternal.

Colossians 3:2 tells us to put our minds on things above, but I love how The Message version of this passage unpacks this:

> If you're serious about living this new resurrection life with Christ, *act* like it. Pursue the things over which Christ presides. Don't shuffle along, eyes to the ground, absorbed with the things right in front of you. Look up, and be alert to what is going on around Christ—that's where the action is. See things from *his* perspective. (vv. 1–2, italics in the original)

You and I both know our lives aren't black and white. It's not earth and then heaven. There's a wild mixing as we live in the now and not yet of life in Christ. We're here, living under the curse of sin and the effects of a fallen world, but the Spirit that raised Jesus Christ from the dead is alive in us.

One last symptom (in this non-exhaustive list) of ignoring death is that we miss the glimpses of eternity here on earth. If we're not looking for heaven to crash in, if we're not expecting His kingdom to come, it still will—we just might not see it.

And what does this have to do with our exhaustion?

If we live in a reality where this is all there is, where we have to work as hard as possible to be as good as we can, and where everything is all death and decay, we'll just keep trying to get through the next few weeks.

You and I were meant and made for so much more than an endless cycle of just getting through the day, over and over again.

We were lovingly made, with creative care, by a Father who placed us here on earth—not as punishment but as praise to Himself. We were placed in His family in an eternal ecosystem where we weren't required to be the energy source or earn our spot. But what's more: We were given roles and rights as His children, His ambassadors, for our joy and His glory—not because He needed drones or nameless soldiers.

Freedom, abundance, healing, joy, and supernatural peace were purchased for us on the cross of Christ. The pain, death, and decay that we experience here on earth isn't final for us; there's more to come. This is just the beginning for us. The end is not something we have to fear—it's where the story gets good.

It's time for us to know (and live into) our place. And it's not running like a hamster on a wheel. We were never created to just get by and keep pushing.

Keeping Rest Realistic

Have you ever heard anyone say, "She's so heavenly minded that she's no earthly good"?

I'm grieved that I've heard someone say it about me. And they didn't invent it. The phrase is attributed to Oliver Wendell Holmes Sr., an associate justice for the Supreme Court who died in 1932. Johnny Cash also added the sentiment to his song called "No Earthly Good." I didn't know Mr. Holmes or Mr. Cash. I'm sure they did a lot of good. But I really don't enjoy this saying or what it implies about people who are caught up in thinking about things above.

I was in college when someone warned me about this attribute of my personality. I remember living for the next few years feeling shame about how deeply and often I thought and talked about God. Looking back, I hate that I wasted so much time feeling condemned for a particular way God made me.

I don't want this book to be so heavenly minded that it's no earthly good. It's imperative to me that you finish the last page feeling like you've got tools and a plan to fight the feeling of tiredness that had you pick it up in the first place. I pray that the insight you find in these pages is practical and realistic and brings you life-changing rest.

So, your promise from me is this: The practical is coming. But first we have to dig into the spiritual side of why we're so tired.

In contrast to Mr. Holmes, C. S. Lewis says that it's the people who have thought a lot about heaven who have done the most for this world.[1] We have to look at heaven to figure out why we're so tired on earth. And doing so will provide us with the mind-changing renewal that will shift our outward lives.

You don't have to keep getting through this week and the next. You were made for and placed into a relationship of rest with God.

You get to practice rest here on earth, under the care of His provision and proof of His presence.

We will experience holy, wild, renewing rest in heaven—and thinking on that now actually helps us share rest here on earth.

Reflection Questions

1. How often do you feel or say that you just need to get through the next few weeks?

2. If you're being honest, what are the main tensions that make you feel that way?

3. How often do you think about death, heaven, and eternity? How does that kind of thinking make you feel?

4. What would it look like for you to live in abundance and freedom now?

Symptoms of Spiritual Exhaustion in Our Lives

- Striving
- Fear that you'll disappoint God or step out of His will
- A distorted or unclear view of the gospel
- Feeling fear or dread about the afterlife
- An inability to receive compassion or give it
- A defeatist mindset about your own life or future

Verses to Meditate On

Psalm 62:1

Truly my soul finds rest in God;
my salvation comes from Him.

Jeremiah 31:25

I will refresh the weary and satisfy the faint.

Romans 8:26–28

In the same way, the Spirit helps us in our weakness. We do not know what we ought to pray for, but the Spirit himself intercedes for us through wordless groans. And he who searches our hearts knows the mind of the Spirit, because the Spirit intercedes for God's people in accordance with the will of God.

And we know that in all things God works for the good of those who love him, who have been called according to his purpose.

six

spiritual exhaustion

"God is with me and for me."

Doing life with people often gives you your own little language with them, you know? For example, my friend Kristen and I always say "ride or die" when referring to our friendship. I don't use that phrase with anyone else, just her. My friend Kalle and I used to say, "Give me all your eggs"—a reference to putting all your eggs in one basket (or not). It was our way of saying, "I'll hold all your stuff—you can trust me."

My son and I made up a term for our friendship: *respecties.* Because one day he was talking about how close we are, almost like besties, and I said, "Yeahhhhh . . . but I still really want you to respect me." It works for us.

My husband, Nick, and I have a phrase that means a lot to us, and this is the origin story. When I got married at age twenty, there were a million books to read on how to be a godly wife. All the "godly wife" books were united on one message: Husbands need physical affirmation and affection. Most of these books focus on this responsibility we have as wives, but very few highlight the importance of receiving physical love as a woman—much less acknowledging the female need for the same kind of attachment.

I went into marriage with a set of expectations about my obligation to give physical touch—never really realizing how important our physical relationship would be to *my* attachment to Nick. I'm very grateful for the thoughtful leadership of Jesus, my husband, and a few wise women to help me unlearn what I'd absorbed. Over time I realized that physical affection is a gift for both of us. I learned that touch is something I can joyfully give and receive, not just give under compulsion. I learned that intimacy unfurls like a flower when you stop demanding particular performances of it.

The excellent news for our relationship was this: The less I felt I had to show physical affection, the more I wanted to. Because I do love my husband, I can't get enough of him. So, when I stopped striving to be the best wife ever, I traded obligation for abundance. And once I understood that our physical connection was for both of us, we enjoyed it a lot more.

And that's around the time we started saying, "This is for me."

Sometimes I'd hug Nick in the middle of the day to thank him for something kind and loving he'd done or just because I wanted him to feel seen and loved. But sometimes I'd hug Nick in the middle of the day because I was craving his affection and comfort. In either situation, after the hug Nick would always say, "Thank you for that hug!" But when I'd come to him out of my own desires and needs, I would say, "Oh, this is for me!"

I wanted him to know (and I tried to remind myself) that I didn't give affection out of obligation. I wanted him to know (and I tried to remind myself) that accessing my desire and need is beautiful and God-honoring. And soon after, he started saying back, "This is for me!" when he'd come in for a hug or grab my hand during a movie. Nothing blesses me more than both of us showing affection from a place of freedom—wanting to love and be loved. Talk about purity. That feels like one of the purest ways we can show up for one another.

Neither of us is taking from the other, but both of us are acknowledging that our covenant allows a freedom to both give affection and receive that same devotion. We can do both: give love selflessly and receive the love we need. That's the power of trust, and it's a power at work in our spiritual lives as well.

You will continue to experience spiritual exhaustion if you believe that every rhythm, every expression of love and service, is only about what God wants or needs from you. You're His daughter and He created you in love, called you in love, redeemed you in love, and longs to keep giving love to you. Not only is it OK for you to need that love, it gives Him glory when you willingly receive it.

I believe that many of us are tired because we're stuck in a cycle of saying, "This is for You," over and over again. Wanting to give God honor and glory is beautiful, but I believe our Father also longs for us to walk into the throne room of grace, get what we need, and say, "This was for me."

One of the most humble, worshipful things we can do as daughters of God is receive what He longs to give—and that includes spiritual rest.

An alternative definition of *exhaustion* is this: constantly doing what you believe everyone else wants or needs from you without ever accessing your desires or needs. Spiritual exhaustion is when we do this with God our Father.

Spiritual Rest

Spiritual exhaustion grows when we begin trading God's care for our obligation, trading God's grace for earning our love, and trading God's abundance for just getting through the day. In that case, we'll need practical ways to embody our identities as daughters who have been purchased into His family. Knowing our place in the kingdom is the antidote to spiritual exhaustion because daughters don't have to work to earn their place, strive to stay relevant, or work for their rest.

I've written previously about how differently women view or picture God when they worship Him. I've told a story about how

I used to imagine Jesus and me riding on horses in the woods, whooshing past trees in pursuit of some enemy. Our talks weren't quiet or reflective. They were shouting and encouraging. But He and I always seemed to be on the go, pushing and fighting and taking new land.

Around the time I started to struggle with my sleep, Holy Spirit began giving me a new picture of the embodied Jesus and me spending time together. I could almost picture Him tying up our horses to a tree while I found somewhere to sit. And with a smile on His face, He'd say, "Why were you riding so fast? Where were you going?"

I want to invite you to sit with Jesus by the tree in this chapter. Maybe it's time for us to unlearn some patterns of pushing and embrace a season of remaining in His presence. Of course, the rhythms we'll peruse as we investigate spiritual rest won't be as tangible as getting more sleep or saying no to new obligations. Still, I know we'll experience healing and hope surging into our souls. Matthew 11:28–30 says,

> Come to me, all you who are weary and burdened, and I will give you rest. Take my yoke upon you and learn from me, for I am gentle and humble in heart, and you will find rest for your souls. For my yoke is easy and my burden is light.

When I first started praying about writing this book, I'd tearfully meditate over this passage with God. Here are a few snippets I wrote in my journal on different days, trying to process and pray through those words of Jesus:

If You're real, I need this to be true.

I won't write this book unless I know this is true.

You said these words. Show me what they mean.

I wouldn't be here and you wouldn't be reading this chapter if I hadn't found some truth and freedom to stand on (or sit on if you're exhausted), but I don't want you to be scared of asking Him to prove them to you as well.

Know Your Place and Bless Your Season

As we seek to "know our place" and find some spiritual rest, let's first get on the same page about the sentiment behind that statement. If someone in everyday life tells you that you need to know or remember your place, they're probably trying to hold you back or stuff you down. There's an inherent pride or arrogance in the insistence that you've somehow wandered outside the boundaries you've been given. That's not what I mean here.

When I say that if we're tired we need to remember our place, I'm speaking of our freedom, wholeness, abundance, and intrinsic identity as daughters of the one true God.

One of the first verses I memorized when I became a believer was Psalm 18:19: "He brought me out into a spacious place; he rescued me because he delighted in me." Something about God's invitation to expansive living, wide-open freedom, and room to run felt like what my soul had been craving my whole life. Before I accepted Jesus at fifteen, walking with God was almost branded as this huge sacrifice: Give up all the fun for the narrow way. So I was deeply surprised and blessed to find that freedom and fun really started when I followed my Savior.

When I talk about our place, I'm talking about how Matthew 5:14 calls us the light of the world. John 1:12 confirms that we're children of God, 1 Peter 2:9 reminds us that we're a royal priesthood, John 15:14–15 calls us friends of Jesus, Romans 8:17 tells us we're heirs of God, 2 Corinthians 5:17 reminds us we're a new creation, 1 Corinthians 3:16 says we're temples of the Holy Spirit . . .

Gals, I could keep going and going.

81

Knowing our place is beautiful, never belittling, in the kingdom of God.

But while we're thinking about psalms and our place, let's read one more verse that is going to lead us to fight exhaustion in a surprising way: "The boundary lines have fallen for me in pleasant places; surely I have a delightful inheritance" (Ps. 16:6).

This verse can be applied in micro ways—by blessing and thanking God for the good things in our lives—but I'd love for us to look at a more macro application and how it helps us fight exhaustion.

I've already told you that every woman I know is tired, but here's a less-talked-about phenomenon: Almost every woman I know feels some sort of insecurity about where she's at in life compared to where she thought she'd be by now. When women receive and believe the message that they're somehow behind, they feel a constant sense of displaced fatigue from unhealthy striving. I know gals who had thoroughly planned to be married at this point, friends who were confident they'd be parents, and friends who are shocked that they're at the start of their second or third careers instead of far along in their first.

I've got friends who anticipated having more stability or savings by this moment. I know women who truly believed they'd still be walking with a particular friend group or community, and they're just not anymore.

Maybe you feel this phenomenon overtly and sharply. Maybe one of those sentences hit you like a punch in the gut, a realization of a lie you've lived under. Or perhaps the tension has just slipped into everything you do, this underlying sense that you're not in the season you are supposed to be in.

An efficient way that you and I can immediately embrace spiritual rest is to recognize these lies and impractical expectations and break ties with their power over our lives. We can know our place as much-loved, creatively made, sustained, and empowered women of God by saying this season right here, whether or not I anticipated it, is exactly where I'm supposed to be. The boundary lines have fallen for me in pleasant places. God is here. Things are growing. I'm not off track or behind, because any of the measurements used to tell me so are created by the world, by culture, and by the enemy of my soul.

Let's make this as practical as possible:

- List any lies or cultural expectations you've believed or agreed with about your current season.
- Ask God for forgiveness and receive the refreshment that comes from repentance.
- Bless your season. Speak out loud or write down some benefits of being in the particular place, space, community, culture, roles, and relationships you're in.

This isn't toxic positivity. I'm not asking you to pretend everything is A-OK and easy peasy. In fact, for the rest of this chapter, we will know our place by accessing our needs, grief, pain, and weaknesses. You don't have to say that it's all great to acknowledge that God hasn't made a mistake placing you exactly where you're at.

Know Your Place and Ask for Wisdom

When we're scanning our lives for the sources of fatigue, many of us will find hours and days spent worrying, wondering, scheming, stressing, and striving. When we tackle mental exhaustion, we'll get into the practicals of what it looks like to bring some rest to our thought lives—but first, we need to acknowledge the spiritual component here, as we are spiritual beings.

When I'm coaching women in their callings, one of my favorite things to remind them is this: We get a leg up because we have access to Holy Spirit.

James 1:5 tells us that God will give us wisdom without reproach if we ask.

Proverbs 2:6 reminds us that the Lord gives wisdom, knowledge, and understanding.

Psalm 51:6 says He makes us know wisdom in the hidden parts.

Colossians 1:9 says we can pray for more wisdom and insight.

Daniel 2:22 declares that God will reveal deep and hidden things to us.

My favorite is Isaiah 30:21, which says, "Whether you turn to the right or to the left, your ears will hear a voice behind you, saying, 'This is the way; walk in it.'"

Knowing our place as daughters of God means that we can trade the spiritual exhaustion that comes from constantly fearing we won't have insight for the confidence of asking and believing we'll receive.

We're also reborn into a family of other believers, which means we can ask for insight and help from humans we trust. We can be humble and admit that we don't have all the information or knowledge we need at a given moment while trusting that God will give us what we need.

I have this theory about prayer that we talk about it more than we actually do it. And so, while asking God for insight might seem super spiritual and not all that helpful, this is where I get to dare us to actually try it.

Praying to our Father and begging Him for wisdom and insight when we're stuck in a cycle of fear, frustration, or confusion is an incredible way to reclaim a little rest in our souls and find the relief we desperately need.

Know Your Place and Rest in the Battle

My daughter made me a fighter. I'm sure the fight was in me all along, but I seemed to misplace it in my twenties. When she was born, I was in a season of great resolve. I had started giving up on dreams, callings, desires, and even passions God had previously given me. And then I birthed this little ball of fight into the world.

Gloriana Eloise is the most tenacious of women, and from an early age she's helped me remember that I can put on the armor of God and live with vibrancy.

But as it goes with little girls who aren't scared of a fight, she often fought my husband and me instead of the world's injustices. Sometimes we were discouraged, and sometimes we'd laugh, but along the way, we started praying that she'd feel the beautiful relief of what Moses speaks to the Israelites in Exodus 14:14: "The LORD will fight for you; you need only to be still."

Something about continually muttering that phrase on her behalf helped me to wonder and want to understand what that would mean for me if I started pausing and waiting before heading into every seemingly important battle that was in front of me.

You may not identify as a fighter, but I'm willing to bet that your mind can conjure some battles that lie in front of you right now. The salvation of people you love, the state of the world, the culture of the church, finding the person you'll marry, the environment, politics, how that random woman on social media was spewing mistruths, the behavior of other people in your life, not to mention your health or the health of those you love. We are in all of these battles (and more), and I'm not advocating for dropping everything in our hands and burying our heads in the sand. Instead I'm saying, with Holy Spirit as our guide, let's each individually hold our hands up and ask, "How am I trying to fight this battle all on my own? Where am I trying to hold back the tide with human hands? Is there any way I could use less energy by trusting that God has got this battle while still worshipfully responding in obedience instead of hiding?"

Maybe it means more prayer and fewer conversations to process with others.

Maybe it means waiting a beat to see if Holy Spirit can work a miracle before you make another move.

Maybe it means picking a verse or a promise of God to recite in the moments when you're prone to practice worry.

Maybe it means learning to walk away from a fight when you realize it is someone's battle but not yours.

You and I will continue to live exhausted if we believe that every battle in front of us depends entirely on our energy, execution, and engagement. Praying, watching, and waiting on God is not our last-ditch effort. It gets to be our first response. Prayer won't be all we do, but it can be the first thing we do. And then, when we're called to action, we'll be sure we're fighting where and what we're meant to, in the name of Jesus.

Know Your Place and Repent

Nothing is more exhausting than pride. And nothing is more common in our culture than pretending to know it all and defending our belief that we've done it all right. I've said it before and I'll say it again: We learn this best by watching reality TV.

How often do we see people on reality TV repeatedly assert, "I'm sorry if that hurt your feelings! My intentions were good!" Um, no, Megan, we watched that whole episode, and your intentions were not good. You were gossiping about Valerie to get Michael mad at her, and it worked. Also, there were cameras on you, so it would work better if you'd just come clean.

OK, that's a funny example, but it's less funny when we do it, which is often.

In contrast, how often do you hear someone completely humble themselves in a conflict? Whether it's a mistake that's been made at work, a spat with a friend, or an argument with a spouse, it's so rare to hear someone say, "I did this on purpose, knowing full well that it would hurt or cost you in some way." And while some tensions and pain points in relationships are accidental and unintentional, not 100 percent are.

Defending yourself is exhausting.

Protecting your image so that no one thinks you ever make a mistake will leave you in burnout.

Fuming because you can't believe they would assume you'd ever do something wrong will bring significant fatigue. I ask this gently: Is it possible part of our tiredness is because we're spending our energy on the wrong things? Is it possible that repentance could be our practice of letting things go and lightening our load?

We're human. We need Jesus. We make mistakes, and we commit sins. We withhold love. We say hurtful things. We don't consider others better than ourselves sometimes. We say something slightly passive in just enough coded language to pretend we didn't mean for it to hurt when really we did. We lose our tempers. We lash out. We hide, and we sometimes lie.

But we get the gospel.

And we get to go to God and say sorry, then go to the humans we hurt and say sorry. And when we do—something wild happens: We experience a grace so compelling we don't want to commit that same sin again. We're changed by grace; we experience refreshment when we repent, and honestly—that's how we change and grow.

> Repent, then, and turn to God, so that your sins may be wiped out, that times of refreshing may come from the Lord, and that he may send the Messiah, who has been appointed for you—even Jesus. (Acts 3:19–20)

It's a beautiful process.

What isn't beautiful is our hearts growing bitter and cold because we falsely assume that being children of God means we will act blameless every day of our lives. Amen?

Know Your Place and Get Brutally Honest with God

During my insomnia breakdown, when I had all but stopped sleeping and walked around like a zombie most days, I got benched from going to church one Sunday.

Nick and I had gone out on a Saturday night, and he asked me how I felt about church the next day. I was pretty numb, numb enough to speak without any kind of filter, and I said, "Does it matter? I have to go anyhow."

I'm so thankful that sentence jarred him. He said, "Wait—hold the phone. You don't have to go. Someone else can take care of your responsibilities. In fact, you can't go. So, stay home, rest if you can, and do whatever you want. But you're taking the day off."

I fought him at first because I, like most women, don't like letting people down. It wasn't until he told me he'd lock me out if I tried to come that I finally gave up. When everyone got up and left, I stayed in my jammies and wandered around the house a little until I finally pulled out my journal.

What unfurled next changed my life, and I didn't see it coming.

I started writing and scribbling as fast as possible, telling God how mad I was at Him. All these issues, the battles I was fighting, and every pocket of my life left me exhausted. He could have fixed it all in one word.

I was tired of raising teens who could have been obedient and easy if He wanted them to be.

I was coaching women fighting against sexism, racism, and wildly negative words spoken to them by people they trusted. He could have fixed that.

I felt the fatigue in my bones from an autoimmune disease that had been wreaking havoc on my body for fifteen years—one glance from Him, and it could have been cured. I was taking care of my body. Where was He?

My friends who were in extreme trauma, where was He for them?

And why in the world did I feel shame about feeling so tired? I'm only human and *He is God*, so couldn't He at least have helped me sleep if He was going to ask me to live this incredibly hard life?

In the rare quiet of being in my house completely alone, I let it all out. I screamed at the ceiling. I may have even used choice words.

And do you know what happened? When it was all said and done and I'd raged my little heart out?

I felt nothing but His compassion for me.

I realized just how much I'd been trying to hold the world over my shoulders when He'd never asked me to do that.

And for every ounce of empathy I carried for others, He held more, and I somehow sensed that as I screamed and prayed.

Trying to keep it tidy with God will leave you tired in a way that nothing else will.

Can I invite you into an honest moment of prayer right now with your Father?

If you're doubtful that spiritual rest will work for you, tell Him now.

If you're struggling with spiritual exhaustion because of the actions or words of someone you trusted, tell God about it.

If you're wondering why He'd allow you to be so burdened and overloaded, let it out.

If you're weary and burdened and can't see where He's at in this, tell Him.

If you're up against the wall and desperate to know what His yoke is, this is the part where you let it out.

Being brutally honest with God and ourselves is the beginning of fighting exhaustion. If it's real rest we want, then we need to get real with God first. This is the first step to moving away from living in a cycle of fatigue that keeps you from the abundance, freedom, and peace that Jesus purchased for you.

Our Father is with you and for you. He created you with care, love, intention, and wild vision. Our Savior and Friend, Jesus, purchased your freedom and abundance on the cross and rose with your healing and resurrection in hand. The Spirit that raised Him from the grave rests on us and works within us to help us see the kingdom of God come in our time.

We are not alone. We are not on the hook or needing to fend for ourselves. God is with us and for us. And this is life-changing news.

Tips for Spiritual Low Power Mode

- Rethink or retool your time with God: If it currently feels like a "have to," switch it up. If it's an intense study time, try reading something a little lighter. If you always feel guilty about not praying longer, try listening to worship music instead. Go on a walk with God. Try journaling, or take a break from journaling.
- Begin a gratitude practice to fight striving about your season.
- Practice saying you're sorry and don't let guilt steal your humility.
- Confess to others to fight shame.

What Women Have to Say

Spiritual exhaustion has looked like not even having the capacity to open my physical Bible for any amount of personal Bible study, even though my desire was there. Mentally and physically, I just did not have it. What helped was realizing God didn't need anything from me to be with me, and while reading Scripture is vitally important, I felt so much freedom in just going on walks with God. Not even praying. Just, in my spirit, asking Him to be with me. In this season I would also just let YouVersion play audio Scripture while I lay down, trusting that His Word would go over me and not return void, even though some moments I couldn't even muster up desire. He was so faithful to keep showing up when I couldn't spiritually.

Rachel, 31, author and social media manager/
copywriter, mom of two, and pastor's wife

seven

physical exhaustion

"I can't just quit."

Here's a humbling but true confession: If I don't go to work to-morrow, the world won't fall apart. Tomorrow, in my office, we've got three meetings: one about an upcoming coaching program, one about onboarding a new employee, and one to plan social media content for the next two weeks. They could probably do all three meetings without me in an emergency and the whole company wouldn't break.

It's almost hard to imagine because sick days aren't really a thing for moms or small business owners. When I got COVID, I still did the dishes (everyone else in the house had it too, so there was no quarantining in my room), and I still recorded one video for social media and one sermon for our church (both from our home). But my point is this: If I took a sick day tomorrow, it would probably be OK.

If I told my kids I couldn't leave my room and didn't tidy, clean, grocery shop, or do laundry for one day, the house wouldn't fall apart. They'd be OK.

If I didn't respond to the text messages from church friends, an-swer my publisher's emails, or meet with my CPA to ensure payroll goes out, everyone would be OK for a day or two. I know my importance in the world; I'm not the cog that keeps the machine working. I can go missing and things won't break apart completely.

And I'm assuming the same is true for you. Everything would be OK for a day or two.

But let's say I didn't show up for another week in any of my roles. Would people be disappointed in me? Yes. Would people potentially lose their income? I think so. Would there be severe consequences for myself and others? There would. If I'm honest, this knowledge used to make me terrified of rest.

I like naming things. Words help me define what I'm feeling and experiencing. And a few years ago, I started calling this clutching feeling of exhausted anxiety from knowing everyone needs me "out on a limb." I feel like I'm out on a fragile limb, and if I yawn, nap, or pause—it will break, and the weight of my fall will hurt me and others.

Maybe you feel out on a limb too. You can't just stop showing up. You can't stop serving, going to work, or taking care of your kids. You can't ignore your aging parents or your child with special needs. You can't stop studying because you're tired, and you can't forget all your friends without hurting some feelings or breaking a relationship.

Our physical presence is essential. But how in the world do we balance that with our genuine need for physical rest and renewal? What do we do when showing up and doing the bare minimum leaves us exhausted in ways we can barely describe? How do we get off the limb, take a breath, and rest?

Your Body Lives in the Kingdom

In my book *Breaking Free from Body Shame*, I talk about having a kingdom mindset. So, let me be honest: Most days, I talk (or at least think) about what it means to have a kingdom mindset. It feels like so much of walking with God is acknowledging "The world is telling me _____, but the kingdom of God preaches _____."

We all probably do this work that Timothy Keller calls "counter-catechizing."[1] When we engage in catechism, we're either instructing or learning the principles of the Christian faith, almost always through question and answer. So, for example, the first question of the Westminster Catechism, which is used in formation and discipleship for many different traditions, is "What is the chief end of man?" Answer: "To glorify God and to enjoy him forever."

Here's what Tim Keller says about counter-catechism: "We need catechesis and counter-catechesis, using biblical doctrine to both deconstruct the beliefs of culture and answer questions of the human heart that culture's narratives cannot."[2]

In my shorthand version, I'd say we need a kingdom mindset. But I also fully agree that we need to hear what the world is telling us and know why it's not true.

We talked in the last chapter about how the truth of heaven impacts our experience on earth, and this truth proves pivotal as it relates to our physical bodies and exhaustion.

If you don't believe in eternity, if this one life that is statistically between seventy and eighty years long is all we get, it would make sense that you'd want to squeeze every second for all it's worth. If you don't believe in eternity, it makes sense to live without limits, maybe even pressing past your physical boundaries to make the most of your time here. If you don't believe in grace or the gospel but believe in an afterlife that you can earn with your goodness, it would make sense to burn the candle at both ends so you can make your way to something better. Or if you're pessimistic and don't believe in eternity, you might conjecture that there are no consequences for anything—so why not burn it all down, including your body, while you're here?

But you and I hold fast to something bigger than ourselves and our understanding. We were purchased into a family by the blood of the King, and our lives were given meaning, calling, and purpose. And our bodies are a part of our whole selves, so it's not just our souls that exist in the kingdom—our bodies can also come into alignment with kingdom truth. By this I mean that the same truths about God, His kindness, His nearness, and His grace that we'd apply to our souls can be applied to our bodies.

We love God in these bodies. We serve God in these bodies. We worship God in these bodies. Our bodies are essentially home base for us until we reach eternity. We love people in these bodies, we experience Holy Spirit in these bodies, and we come into agreement with God's will in these bodies.

I use the phrase *agreement* a good bit when it comes to kingdom principles, and for me it essentially means this: acknowledging that God's way is good for me and lining up my life in a way that looks like I believe it. It's the fulfillment of being a person who is not just a hearer of God's Word but also a doer (James 1:22).

We've already established that we live in the now and not yet. We're placed in rest, given space to practice God's rest on earth, but we're ultimately headed somewhere much better—an eternal and perfect rest with our Father.

When we apply that good news (that we're headed for ultimate rest) to our bodies, take a deep breath, and look at the physical implications of our spiritual reality, I believe we'll find some comforting and compelling truths. We won't want to stay tired, and we'll have access to wisdom about breaking this cycle.

The grace of God will keep us from pushing our bodies to the limits to serve and to earn our place in the kingdom.

The compassion of God will keep us from disassociating from our bodies and pretending they don't need care.

The nearness of God will help us experience peace and patience in a way that makes rest not just practical and accessible but life-giving and life-changing.

Our spiritual realities will shift the way we experience God in the physical if we allow ourselves to be transformed by the renewing of our minds.

Our bodies live in the kingdom, but the default pace of this world is killing us. If we don't counter-catechize or dismantle the breakneck momentum that we're born into on earth, we'll spin right into exhaustion and stay there for the rest of our lives. If we keep believing the lie that we just can't quit, even for a moment, the pace will prevail. Some level of exhaustion is what we're subject to here on earth, but there's a layer of striving and speed that we don't have to keep consenting to.

Our bodies live in the kingdom. So let's find out what a kingdom pace looks like right where we're at.

You Don't Have to Consent

I'm not great at texting. I used to try and assure people, "It's me, not you!" I love my friends, family, and acquaintances, but I just can't keep up with text messages. But as time passes, I'm even more careful not to blame myself anymore. I want to be clear: I love a text message. A good emoji or GIF, a long update when a friend asks me how a particular meeting or moment went. I love texting my teens when I'm away for work. I love the ease. I love the connection. I love words!

But the truth is, I could text forty hours a week and never really feel like I've caught up. Because when you start answering texts and engaging, they just keep coming back. They're like word boomerangs that catch the wind before you catch your breath.

I do what I can, but I will not put myself on the hook to answer immediately every hour of the day. So prepare yourself for a tiny rant that I find myself giving anytime someone says I'm bad at texting.

When did we decide to be reachable twenty-four hours a day by anyone with something to say? When did we consent? When did we agree to be more "connected" electronically and less connected to our souls? Is it when I got my first cell phone? Or when the iPhone made texting that much easier? Do I consent monthly when I pay my bill?

While I'm ranting, I'd like to add that when I pay for something, I hope it helps me, not hurts me. But if I'm paying a fee each month that requires me to always be accessible, I'd rather not pay it. Thanks. I mean, I will. Because it's the right thing to do, and again, I like to text my kids. But I'm sure going to rant about it when the time is right.

So now what I do (when I'm not ranting) is find appropriate moments to alert people in my life to my boundaries with electronics. I clarify that they can do whatever is right for them, but I may not respond immediately if the issue isn't urgent. I'm not trying to be impolite or unkind. I'm just going at the pace that is sustainable for me.

And I'm hoping it catches on. I always remind my friends they don't have to apologize for not texting me back immediately.

I'm just one person here. But what if we all changed? What would happen if entire people groups, communities, and families decided they no longer wanted to consent to a pace that was unsustainable?

What if we said no thanks and normalized knowing what our souls need—even if it goes against cultural norms? What if we stopped apologizing and pretending like it's our problem that we can't keep up with a speed that we were never meant to be able to withstand? And what if we asked some honest questions about who is promoting this pace we're all casually consenting to?

What I'm saying is, in the places of pressure where we often feel we don't have a choice, we do. It might run counter to what's normal, what's expected, and it might raise some eyebrows, but God always makes a way for our peace, should we choose to follow it.

It might not be texting for you, but you get to exercise authority and autonomy to know where you need physical limits and boundaries.

You have the freedom to say no to invitations that would cause you fatigue if you said yes. You can leave the dishes in the sink and the laundry in the hamper if it means getting in a quick nap to catch up after a sleepless night. You can ask for help instead of insisting on doing it all yourself to seem strong and independent. You can show up to the holiday empty-handed if the hostess has told you she's got it covered. You can ask for an extension or a rain check if exhaustion has crept up on you.

You and I might not be able to quit everything, to stop showing up in all the areas of our lives, but we can set limits and draw boundaries. We've been given that capacity and authority in our own lives.

Go Slow Enough to be Loved by God

If we're wondering how in the world we'll start finding a kingdom pace, let's start at the best part: being loved by God.

A few years ago, when I was in the thick of my most tired season, I decided to study Psalm 23. It seemed so peaceful, and I was curious to see if the words would help me feel more rested and restful.

> The LORD is my shepherd, I lack nothing.
>   He makes me lie down in green pastures,
> he leads me beside quiet waters,
>   he refreshes my soul.
> He guides me along the right paths
>   for his name's sake.
> Even though I walk
>   through the darkest valley,
> I will fear no evil,
>   for you are with me;
> your rod and your staff,
>   they comfort me.
>
> You prepare a table before me
>   in the presence of my enemies.
> You anoint my head with oil;
>   my cup overflows.

Surely your goodness and love will follow me
    all the days of my life,
and I will dwell in the house of the LORD
    forever.

What I notice most immediately when reading these words of David is the kindness, compassion, and intimacy with which he describes God the Father. And if I'm honest, the second thing I notice is that I feel shame about rarely lying in green pastures or sitting beside quiet waters. Part of this I come by honestly because I'm a seriously *indoorsy* kind of girl. I love a mall. And I love looking at nature, but I think I love it most when I'm looking through a window from a comfy sofa with my air conditioned to a perfect seventy degrees.

Anyhow, I see myself as this too-busy problem child who won't ever just sit down and settle with God. But what if we turn this passage around and see another self-fulfilling problem that keeps being perpetuated in most of our lives?

What if the question is not, Why can't we slow down long enough to love God well? What if instead we ask, Are we going slow enough to let ourselves be loved by God?

One question leaves us striving and feeling shame. The other leaves us feeling loved by the God who created the universe. That kind of love compels us to get in His presence *more*, which in this situation means we'd be slowing down and resting to receive more of His love.

Sorry, I love questions. Last ones—promise: What if a core motivation behind our hurried and hectic pace is our desire to earn God's love? And what if consenting to a slower pace was a defiant way we could agree with the good news of the gospel?

Before revamping your task list and your time management, before resetting your rhythms, before any quitting decisions are made, let's ask the questions beneath all the problems.

What would it look like for you to go slow enough to be loved by God?

What would it look like for you to go slow enough to be comforted by God?

What would it look like for you to get a little ranty and tell the world, "It's not me. It's you. I can't keep saying yes, doing more, and going faster. I need to be led by my Father to the still waters. I need my soul restored"?

You wake in the morning, and as the to-do list begins assaulting you and the shame of not getting it all done yesterday creeps up, you push those thoughts aside to spend a little time reading and praying. Not because God needs you to or because you're trying to earn anything but because you'd rather start your day knowing you're loved instead of knowing you're caught up on the never-ending list of tasks.

When presented with an opportunity to serve, you take the time to ask God if this is something He's inviting you to do or if it's for someone else. You have nothing to prove to Him or anyone else about your righteousness.

You notice the dishes before going to bed but forgo actually washing them because your worth isn't tied up in the cleanliness of your sink. You used to believe the lie that you just had to have this done to rest, and now you know you can daringly take God's invitation, even when everything isn't finished.

Maybe you start putting your office hours in your email signature to signal to people when you will and won't respond. You no longer believe the lie that you have to be constantly accessible to be a great leader or friend. Instead, you know that soaking up God's goodness in your life and being loved well by Him equips you to be who He made you when you do lead, serve, and love others.

Allowing ourselves to be loved by God will have a domino effect in our lives, catapulting us into a consistent craving for His love and comfort. In the next chapter, we'll talk about the practicals of slowing our pace, but we'll never be able to make it happen if we don't want it.

Nothing will make us want a kingdom pace more than the aftereffect of allowing ourselves to be loved by God.

We need to go slow enough to be loved by God, not slow enough to please God or make Him love us. That ship has sailed with our Savior at the helm. We're loved. We're accepted. "There is therefore now no condemnation for those who are in Christ Jesus" (Rom. 8:1 ESV).

Go Slow Enough to Hear and See God

A lot of being a business owner and boss is foreign to me. To lead my team at Go + Tell Gals, I have to google a lot and ask questions anytime someone who knows about business and leadership is willing to share their insights. But one piece of leadership that was instinctive for me was setting team culture.

Our team culture is simply a written guide verbally outlining *how* we work. It reminds us of who we are, who we want to be.

From the get-go, we had one culture point that I want to invite you into as well: We go slow enough to see and hear God.

As the leader of our business, I know we have a leg up as kingdom women because there is no effort in which we work alone. We can pray and ask God for insight. We can be inspired by the awe that comes from a life of worship. We can watch how God is moving in the lives of other women and direct our efforts toward serving them. We can be compelled by the grace, power, and presence of Jesus and press through challenging circumstances.

But we can't do any of it if we're not going slow enough to watch and listen. And I wrote this culture point knowing my propensity to settle into a pace that denotes that I've forgotten I live in the kingdom. And while Holy Spirit lives inside me, if I'm going too fast and the world is too noisy, my voice will drown out the small one that whispers kingdom promise and peace.

For me, in my personal life, going slow enough to see and hear God looks like this:

- I make time to have a gratitude practice.
- I take the margin I need before making decisions.
- I have time at night and in the morning to reflect on the past or the coming day.
- I'm not so busy on the weekends that I find myself distracted and sleepy on Sunday morning during church.
- My schedule has enough margin for me to be spontaneous in serving others.

We need a pace that helps us see what God is doing and hear what He's speaking.

Jesus talks to His disciples about this in Matthew 13:

"Whoever has ears, let them hear."

The disciples came to him and asked, "Why do you speak to the people in parables?"

He replied, "Because the knowledge of the secrets of the kingdom of heaven has been given to you, but not to them. Whoever has will be given more, and they will have an abundance. Whoever does not have, even what they have will be taken from them. This is why I speak to them in parables:

"Though seeing, they do not see;
   though hearing, they do not hear or understand.

In them is fulfilled the prophecy of Isaiah:

"'You will be ever hearing but never understanding;
   you will be ever seeing but never perceiving.
For this people's heart has become calloused;
   they hardly hear with their ears,
   and they have closed their eyes.
Otherwise they might see with their eyes,
   hear with their ears,
   understand with their hearts
and turn, and I would heal them.'

But blessed are your eyes because they see, and your ears because they hear." (vv. 9–16)

I can't imagine anything more devastating than getting to the end of my life and realizing it was too full to see and hear what was happening in the kingdom. I can't imagine the regret I'd feel upon meeting Jesus in eternity to realize He had been talking and showing me so much on earth, but the pace of my life had drowned it out.

The pace of our culture tells us to keep our heads down and press in. The pace of the kingdom says, "Look up and listen! Take a breath and hear what the King of heaven has to say."

Go Slow Enough to Love Others

A few years ago, Holy Spirit convicted me with one phrase that I couldn't get out of my head: There's a difference between loving people and wanting to seem like you're loving. At the time, I'd built a life that looked like it was very loving. But the truth is, it was too full for me to connect with my own emotions or desires to love well. So instead I was going through the motions, loving people with my body and feeling bitter and disconnected in my heart.

There's no doubt that a kingdom pace, a kingdom life, will call us to sacrifice and serve others. Consider these verses:

My command is this: Love each other as I have loved you. Greater love has no one than this: to lay down one's life for one's friends. (John 15:12–13)

Carry each other's burdens, and in this way you will fulfill the law of Christ. (Gal. 6:2)

Do nothing out of selfish ambition or vain conceit. Rather, in humility value others above yourselves, not looking to your own interests but each of you to the interests of the others. (Phil. 2:3–4)

I don't think any of you are seeking permission for a toxic version of self-care that promotes a life where you nurture and notice only your own needs. You are women who want to love well. You live a life of seeing and serving others. But what if your pace is preventing you from loving with sincerity? And what if your pace is leading to a level of physical exhaustion that's leaving you at risk for burnout?

As we're looking at the way of Jesus, the pace of Jesus, and trying to chase down what He's saying as He promises a way that isn't weary or heavy laden, let's look at His life. If I asked you what Jesus did in His three years of earthly ministry, I wonder what would be on everyone's list:

He healed so many.

He listened to people.

He taught endlessly.

He prayed.

He ate with people.

He attended celebrations.

He engaged with religious and political leaders.

But what about the list of things Jesus didn't do? Here are just a few of the passages that give me some insight into a kingdom pace that will help me love people well:

Immediately Jesus made the disciples get into the boat and go on ahead of him to the other side, while he dismissed the crowd. After he had dismissed them, he went up on a mountainside by himself to pray. (Matt. 14:22 23)

Rising very early before dawn, he left and went off to a deserted place, where he prayed. (Mark 1:35 NABRE)

But the Pharisees and the teachers of the law were furious and began to discuss with one another what they might do to Jesus.

One of those days Jesus went out to a mountainside to pray, and spent the night praying to God. (Luke 6:11–12)

Some time after this, Jesus crossed to the far shore of the Sea of Galilee (that is, the Sea of Tiberias), and a great crowd of people followed him because they saw the signs he had performed by healing the sick. Then Jesus went up on a mountainside and sat down with his disciples. (John 6:1–3)

The pace of Jesus involves withdrawing when needed, resting and living inside the physical limitations of an earthly body, occasionally saying no to people in need, and prioritizing intimacy with God and others. Does that mean that He wasn't loving? Of course not. So, we can only conclude that by honoring boundaries and physically resting, Jesus was enabled to love people well.

Ultimately, for you and me to live a life of love and sacrifice, we've got to go slow enough to love ourselves and God well so that we can also love others for the long haul.

We Can't Just Quit, But...

You and I can't just quit every responsibility or role that we're called to. And thankfully, breaking the cycle of fatigue and exhaustion doesn't mean we have to drop everything. However, following Jesus as He shows us the free and light way will mean accepting a kingdom pace for our lives. It will look different for each of us based on our particular bodies, seasons, needs, and roles.

But if we're tired of being tired, a shift in our pace is probably the most important place we can start.

If the only hope for our breaking free of exhaustion were to clear out our lives, I'd imagine we'd all feel pretty hopeless. But if we continually accept the reactive defeat that tells us, "It's always going to be this way," nothing will change, and our fatigue will only get worse.

Can I tell you a secret?

I have one secret hope for every book I write, no matter the subject. I hope and pray that after women put my books down, they feel more equipped to hear from God than they did when they started reading. And the same is true for this book.

I wish I could sit with you and a blank whiteboard, detailing every responsibility in your life and helping you discern what needs to stay and what needs to go. But the great news is this: I know our Father is a better communicator than I am, and I know He wants to help you sort through your life to figure out what can be taken off your plate and what needs to be shifted for more rest.

You can't just quit it all, but compelled by the love of God, you can change your pace. You can find sustainable rhythms that help you fight the fatigue that will inevitably come as you live under the effects of this fallen world. You can change the way you make decisions, the way you live and lead, and the ways you rest.

Let's go slow enough to remember we live in the kingdom.

Let's go slow enough to see and hear God.

Let's go slow enough to love others.

And most importantly, let's slow down so we can receive the love our Father is trying to give us.

Reflection Questions

1. How do you feel about your current pace? Is it sustainable, life-giving, or exhausting?
2. What are the main factors influencing your current pace of life?
3. What are the main barriers keeping you from shifting your pace?
4. What would it look like to invite God to speak into your pace?

Symptoms of Physical Exhaustion in Our Lives

- Yawning, headaches, dizziness, sore muscles
- Saying yes because no one else will
- Always arriving early or staying late out of obligation
- Sleep sabotage: staying up later than is wise to get time for yourself
- Moodiness or irritability
- Feeling like you can't be fully present

Verses to Meditate On

Proverbs 3:24

When you lie down, you will not be afraid;
when you lie down, your sleep will be sweet.

Exodus 33:14

The LORD replied, "My Presence will go with you, and I will give you rest."

Psalm 127:2

It's useless to rise early and go to bed late,
and work your worried fingers to the bone.
Don't you know he enjoys
giving rest to those he loves? (MSG)

eight

physical exhaustion

"My limitations are not a liability."

"Why do you keep saying that word? What do you mean when you say it?"

I was sitting at dinner with a mentor, a woman who also writes books and leads in a public capacity. My husband and the co-founder of Go + Tell Gals, Anna, were at the table with us. The question, however, was directed at me.

And the word I kept repeating was *autonomy*.

To be honest, I had been saying it for months. It had been slipping out of my mouth in vulnerable moments, but I wasn't quite sure what I meant when I said it either. I just knew that I didn't feel like I had it. There was a void in my life where I was craving autonomy.

I'm the kind of person who thinks in story, so when this mentor asked what I meant by autonomy, all I could think of were stories in which I realized I didn't have it. At the time, in my mind, autonomy meant having a healthy sense of boundaries and borders. Autonomy meant knowing where I ended and everyone else began. But again, I could describe the poignant moments where I could sense its absence more than large portions of my life where it was present.

I thought about the time I got COVID. It was in the thick of the pandemic before the general terror wore off, and I was terrified. Once I made it past the contagious days, I decided my body needed a gentle walk, and I put on my tennis shoes and charted a short path around my neighborhood. My breathing was still not back to normal, my limbs felt weak and fatigued, but I knew I needed to move to feel healthy again.

For a few months I'd been living in paralyzing fear about what I'd do if someone I loved got sick. I'd made emergency plans, researched vitamins and supplements, and constantly texted everyone I knew with the words "Wellness check!" When I was sick, I had friends and family who checked in on me, but none of them seemed panicked. All of them seemed to understand that they could pray for me, encourage me, and hope for the best . . . but that was it. So, what was up with me feeling like everyone else's health was my responsibility? My physical burden to carry? Why did I innately feel like someone would blame me if they got sick?

Another memory: I thought about how one of my teens had recently struggled intensely with depression and anxiety. Pain, frustration, and terror gripped me because I knew these struggles as my own in the past. I wanted to save them from this heartache, even though I knew the healing that would ultimately come would lead to their victory. But more than wanting to rescue them from the pain—inwardly, I wanted to be the solution. I realized over time that I believed (falsely) that if I prayed enough, made the right meals, had a cheery enough voice, encouraged the right strategies, hugged at the right time, and provided exactly what this child needed with my own body, they'd get better.

But parenting is never that simple, and neither are mental health struggles. Sure, I could be a present mother—pray and encourage, provide support and compassion—but my body could not fix what this child's body was feeling. Ultimately, there is a point where I end and they begin.

Another memory floated to my mind: My two best friends had recently had their first babies in a one-week time span. My two best friends! Birthed their first babies! In the same week! My soul was elated—these were women I'd known for years and felt so much closeness with. I pictured myself cuddled with each of them in their hospital beds after the babies were born, standing over the bassinet in the middle of the night helping calm a fussy newborn, and commiserating over the lack of sleep together. You can laugh at my lack of boundaries, but I promise you these pictures were created in love! I love these women, and I wanted to do motherhood with them!

They both patiently helped me reevaluate my unhelpful expectations before they went into labor, but a deep grief came over me in the weeks that followed the births. I felt like these two friends, these two new moms, *needed* me. For the fussy nights, the awe-inspiring cuddle sessions, and the retelling of the labor woes. My body didn't quite know how to handle the suspended animation of thinking about the babies and their moms so much without actually being physically present at all times.

Until one day I went over to my friend Kristen's house and saw her holding her newborn and it hit me: She didn't need me in order to become a mom. It was in her all along, and God was giving her what she needed. I got to watch and encourage, but I wasn't a part of the process.

Maybe these stories feel extreme to you, and that's OK. Some of this is just who I am. Being a cheerleader for those I love is my superpower. But when it's taken too far, it can look like a struggle with autonomy. Looking back now, I can see that I was losing the boundaries and borders of my own self as the lines blurred with compassion and care for others. I was so wrapped up in everyone else's health that I couldn't quite find where I ended and they began.

There was a time in my life when I'd been a person who thought and even taught about boundaries a good deal. I wasn't perfect at living a boundaried life, but I had drawn some helpful ones in the past. I knew how to say no to some degree. But when my own exhaustion overwhelmed me, I felt like I'd lost my capacity to detach myself from others compassionately. I was losing autonomy.

I noticed myself taking empathy to an extreme level in every relationship or sphere I was in. If someone in my life was hurting, I was hurting too. If someone had a need, I felt personally responsible for meeting it. If someone wasn't living free in my midst, I thought it my responsibility to crawl into whatever pit they were in so we could climb out together.

My time, my emotions, my spiritual health, my thought life, and even my body—it all felt like a communal experience. I had lost autonomy.

Flash forward a year and a half. I'd had a mental breakdown due to exhaustion and was inching my way back to physical and mental wholeness, and this wise woman sitting across from me was asking what I meant every time I said, "I need to get my autonomy back."

When I confirmed that I wasn't quite sure what I was saying, it was time to do some research.

Autonomy is an interesting word because it means both authority and freedom. The authority side of autonomy is self-government. It indicates that the subject has the capacity to make decisions and determine what's needed. But within autonomy, there's also liberty—the freedom to feel, move, desire, and go where needed.

As I studied the word, I realized I hadn't lost my autonomy. I'd just traded it. No one was taking or demanding my authority or freedom, but I'd willingly given it up because I thought that was what loving others required of me.

To be honest, as a believer who loves God's Word and loves receiving teaching, I've heard mixed reviews on how much autonomy we should be seeking anyhow. I've heard whole messages emphasizing our dependence on God and eschewing our need for independence. I've always heard incredible teaching on community and our interdependence in the kingdom. I actually don't see these messages as conflicting, but rather multiple sides of the same diamond—all illuminating the light of heaven and the way we're created in love.

We need God, and we shouldn't ever try to escape that; rather, surrendering to our need for Him is where we find freedom and healing.

We need one another, to rely on each other and walk together as we walk with God.

But we also need to understand where our limitations and boundaries begin and end. And in my situation, no one was necessarily bulldozing over my personal borders—no one but me.

Over time, I reestablished my body's beautiful God-given boundaries and borders of autonomy. I began to listen to my body's cues about fatigue, hunger, fear, and overwhelm. I started to make wise decisions about my capacity *before* I felt exhausted, leaving margin and space to rest first. I still get tripped up sometimes and begin to believe the lie that loving people requires me to release my limits, but it's easier to come back to the center of what's suitable for my soul and my body.

A significant shift came for me when I realized that, from a kingdom perspective, autonomy is agreeing with the authority God has given me to steward the life He has given me. He's given me the capacity to care for my own spirit, mind, and relationships—and also my body. No one else can do it for me. And when I care for my body by nourishing it, resting it, and recognizing my limits, I do the will of God. His kingdom comes when His will is done, and His will is done when I nurture the body He's given me. Suddenly self-care, resting, and saying no—none of these are selfish. They're the basis for my giving God glory and being able to care for others.

No One Taught Us

We're getting wiser in so many ways as a society. One of my favorite shifts we've made as a whole is that in most communities it's no longer acceptable to make your kids hug or receive hugs from strangers. As for me, I am 100 percent touchy-feely to the max when I feel safe and comfortable. If I don't feel secure—emotionally, mentally, or physically—it's a hard no. Don't lay a finger on me. This means, even if you're my husband or best friend, if I'm crying or scared—hands off.

When I was growing up, we weren't so evolved about the physical boundaries of kids. No one was. And I remember feeling so uncomfortable with the expectation that any adult who wanted to could hug me, and I'd have to reciprocate it. There is a myriad of reasons why it's so important that we give kids the security to choose who touches them, but one of the most basic is this: It teaches them that boundaries, especially physical ones, are healthy to establish and keep. Unfortunately for most of us, no one taught us this. And now, as adults, we live in a culture where it's become increasingly more acceptable to respect boundaries—but we still have so far to go.

On top of the fact that we weren't taught about our authority to steward and nourish our bodies, many of us have extenuating circumstances that prohibit us from feeling like our bodies are ours. Sickness, chronic illness, aging, injury, and pervasive body shame can lead to a profound disconnection from our bodies. The longer we feel like something outside of our control is happening to us, the more intensely we'll struggle to feel connected to our flesh.

Motherhood and marriage are incredible blessings that can also cause us to struggle with autonomy. First, there's the complex one-flesh theology of marriage that leads many of us to forget that while we share a connection physically with our spouses, we do so willingly—not under compulsion. In Ephesians 5, Paul calls this theology a mystery, but this is true: We can become one flesh and still maintain our individual spiritual and physical autonomy. For example, if your husband is in sin, you do not need to confess. That is his sin, and vice versa. If you become pregnant and find yourself in labor, it would be frustrating to hear him complain about the contractions when he's just standing beside you. Amen?

We're one flesh, but two individual spiritual and physical beings. In fact, our unity is sweetened and our connection is deepened when we recognize our own boundaries and borders and make space for our spouses in love.

In the miracle of motherhood, we get the honor of using our bodies to nurture others, no matter how a child enters our family. But this role can blur the lines between where we begin and our children end. And again, there just isn't a plethora of teaching that encourages mothers to practice autonomy by caring for their bodies as they care for others. Some of the assumptions and burdens that we as a culture have placed on women are getting better, but still—we're up against centuries of the unspoken expectation that a woman is meant to be a giver even at personal expense.

We are praised for pushing past our physical limitations as wives, mothers, students, and friends. We're labeled as strong when we ignore our own physical needs over and over again without processing the ramifications for this continued denial of our God-given boundaries.

Spiritual and physical abuse, career expectations, technology, mental illness, the breakneck speed of culture, and the objectification of women—all of these are societal factors that encourage and enable a disconnection from our bodies.

But here's the excellent news: Reconnecting with our bodies, with Holy Spirit as a guide, will deepen our spiritual life and help us fight exhaustion. Reembracing our limitations and relearning the boundaries and borders of our bodies is not even slightly selfish. It's God-glorifying. And it will enable us to serve, love, and lead well for the long haul.

A Word on Hustle

Hustle has gotten a bad rap the past few years—and honestly, it's probably for a good reason. The phrase *hustle culture* has become more widely known in the past decade, but the values behind it have been around much longer. The ideology of hustle culture is rooted in the notion that pushing, striving, and working harder, potentially at personal cost, is an admirable way to pursue success. Hustle culture glorifies the success that comes through sacrifice. Unfortunately, the romanticism behind this idea is often betrayed by reality. Because even when we hustle our way to the top, we quickly find there's no rest for us there either—we have to keep pushing and pushing to maintain our momentum in a never-ending endeavor.

A few years ago at an event, I heard author and communicator Jon Acuff say, "Hustle has a season." At the time, he was speaking to other entrepreneurs and authors, and I appreciated the point he was making. Particularly in the entrepreneurial world, some periods are appointed for building whatever you're launching. It may mean working nights and weekends to transition away from another job or performing multiple roles before you're able to hire someone. What I loved most about what Jon said is that while there's a place for pushing hard, you can't keep going that way forever.

I'm not even slightly a fan of hustle culture or the glamorization of denying our own physical needs to earn success. But I am incredibly aware that in our lives there are seasons where more is required of us physically, emotionally, and mentally. Normal rhythms of rest and renewal won't work for us in those seasons. In those times, there is no choice but to persevere for various reasons.

Whether it's caring for a sick family member, going back to grad school, starting a new business, nursing a new baby, or going through a huge life transition, there are periods in our lives that are not normal. In that case, hustle has a season. I don't think the presence of these conditions means that we can't or won't experience rest—instead, it means we may have to work more creatively to meet our physical needs. But identifying these moments as being out of the ordinary is critical so we don't begin to think of them as typical. Momentary or temporary seasons of pushing harder than normal need to be seen as the exception to the rule, and it's so incredibly wise and helpful to know this: Sometimes the best thing about seasons is that they all eventually end.

A Word on Defeat

The idea of autonomy is that we have the freedom and authority to make decisions that keep us healthy and whole. The power of autonomy is that no one can take it from us. The beauty of autonomy is that the more we accept this liberty we've been given and walk with Holy Spirit to use it worshipfully, the more intimacy we'll experience with God and others.

Autonomy also means we can choose self-compassion because our human limitations are not a liability from our Father's perspective. God isn't disappointed that your body needs rest; He made you with intentionality and purpose—and He is not surprised that you cannot continually push past your own physical boundaries.

It's important to note that the real enemy of autonomy is defeat.

Discouragement is when we feel dismayed or frustrated about the way something is. For example, if you feel discouraged about the state of your life and the lack of physical rest you're currently experiencing, that can be a healthy first step to experiencing lasting change.

Defeat is when we feel hopeless in addition to being discouraged, and it can be almost impossible to experience renewal if we're agreeing with defeat and asserting that it's always going to be this way.

I pray that in this book, you sense the nearness of God as He lovingly leads you to find realistic rest for your body, mind, and soul. And it's with that desire that I invite you to pay attention to any defeat you might feel about your exhaustion. If you are sensing some agreement in your spirit with the lie that says it will always be this way, that you'll always be tired no matter what, I completely understand how you got there. But I'm going to lovingly invite you to confess that to God so we can see if some fresh hope might not help us fight the fatigue we've been battling for so long.

If you're willing to come with me, with even a shred of hope, let's keep going.

Find Your Edges

Here's a fun fact: Even the widely accepted eight hours of sleep was a manufactured guesstimate made during the industrial revolution. With the invention of the eight-hour workday, there was an encouragement to divide your day into eight hours of work, eight hours of recreation, and eight hours of sleep.

Arbitrary expectations of rest aren't going to help us fight exhaustion. Instead, we need individual exploration of our own physical needs. We need trial and error to determine how our bodies get the renewal they need so we can first rest and then love, serve, lead, and enjoy life.

I have one friend who has to have nine to ten hours of sleep. She's a new mom who is now navigating this season with the full awareness that she needs help to get back to that target as soon as possible. So she'll say no to fun events, she'll leave a party early, she doesn't watch TV at night, and she does not ever touch caffeine—because she knows this need her body has to function at its best.

I have another friend who's worked incredibly hard to figure out how to maintain two consecutive days off from work a week, even though she works retail and the schedule shifts each week. She doesn't mind going in late, moving around her Sabbath, or missing community events. She knows her body needs the full forty-eight hours disengaged from production to be renewed.

Another woman I know is determined to experience Sabbath even though she has nine kids. Laundry, dishes, vacuuming, and carpooling are all on her "no" list for twenty-four hours one day each week. These are her boundaries and borders.

After exploring my own need for physical rest over the past few years, I've found a variety of rhythms and rules that work for me:

- I need one hour of quiet in the morning before I have to interact with other people or leave my house. I'll get up at the crack of dawn to do this if I have to.
- After high-impact days (travel, public speaking, exciting or tense moments) that require a lot of my nervous system, sweet potatoes and salmon are the foods that help my adrenal system function normally again.
- I shower every night before bed and make it a whole process. First, as previously mentioned, I watch TV (propping my phone up away from the water) in the shower. Then, I take a few minutes to myself in the warmth, sipping the large glass of ice water I usually bring in.
- I can't sit too still on my days off. I need to move my body because that's how I'm best recreated in moments of rest.

These are just a few examples, but this is my point: Only you can figure out and determine your personal borders and boundaries, and then only you can create rhythms in your life that honor them. So, think of this less as a task looming over you and more as an opportunity to reconnect with who God made you to be, to listen to and learn from the beautiful limitations of your body so you can honor them worshipfully.

Here are some questions to get you started:

- How much sleep is optimal for you in this season?
- Can you begin setting a standard bedtime routine and hour to honor the biblical principle of evening and then morning, rest then work?
- What food and exercise practices leave you feeling renewed?
- Where do you most need quiet and time to regroup in your day? How can you work that in?
- Where can you build in rhythmic rest weekly, quarterly, and yearly?

Saying No

Ladies, there's no getting around it. I wish there was another way, for all of our sakes. But unfortunately, if we're going to stop living tired, specifically physically exhausted, we'll have to learn how to say no. If we're struggling to find adequate physical rest at our current level of commitments, we have to have fewer commitments.

And for most of us, there's just too much: too many opportunities, invitations, and options. Even if your life feels void of communal invitations, your presence in our current culture means you've got an onslaught of choices being hurled at you constantly. The TV choices we have access to alone mean we will have to say no. Sister, you can't watch every show people are talking about. There's no time!

Finding the physical rest you need may mean saying no to baking for that upcoming event, hosting book club or the committee meeting, stepping up to serve because someone else canceled, or organizing the family reunion.

Let's cover some of the many reasons we hate saying no, and then let's make a logistical plan to face our fears and start sending our regrets without regret.

- *We don't like to say no because we don't want to disappoint people.* Galatians 1:10 always gets me in the gut: "Am I now trying to win the approval of human beings, or of God? Or am I trying to please people? If I were still trying to please people, I would not be a servant of Christ." I know we like making people happy, but at the end of the day, continually allowing ourselves to be people pleasers is an idol-worship issue. We've got to confess this to God, repent, and turn away.

  What's more, I've found that most people don't want you to say yes out of obligation. One more thing to hit here: You are potentially robbing someone else of the opportunity to say yes to the thing you're doing begrudgingly. If you're saying yes because of people-pleasing, say no in Jesus's name.

- *We don't like to say no because we don't want to miss out.* Friends, I'm sorry to speak so plainly, but I've learned not to play nice with sin. The "fear of missing out" may not seem sinister, but at its root we'll often find a deficit of gratitude in our own lives. FOMO is a struggle with contentment that needs to be confessed and repented of, not treated as if it's a normal label to write over our lives.

  Gratitude says, "I'm thankful for what I have right here," and generosity says, "I'm thankful for what you have over there." Will we still occasionally feel the pain of missing out? Sure. Will we change our availability based on it? Maybe let's don't. If you're saying yes because of FOMO, say no in Jesus's name.

- *We don't like to say no because we ask, "If I don't, who will?"* As a result, we feel responsible and on the hook for the people we love or want to show up for. This tension is so real and honest, but it's still a great moment to check where our faith and beliefs are rooted. If we don't get the report done, who will? If we don't do the laundry, who will? If we don't volunteer to be classroom mom, who will? If we don't lead the meeting, who will? Sometimes we're so confident that we're the only ones who can be trusted that we forget to trust God. In a moment, I'm going to share a story that changed my life regarding feeling responsible. But for now, I'll just remind you: If you're saying yes because you believe you're the only one who can be counted on, say no in Jesus's name.

Now, how in the world will we say no?

1. We'll say no bravely as leaders, believing that we're making space for more women to honor their own limitations and boundaries.

2. We'll say no without apologizing. If you're used to profusely saying you're sorry when you decline an invitation, this will take practice. But by abstaining from an apology, you help remind yourself and others that you're not doing anything wrong.

3. We'll say no right when we know it's a no. We won't hyperspiritualize it (by saying we're praying about it) or string people along (if it's a no, it's a no).

4. We won't lie about our availability or whether or not we can try and make it work.

5. Finally, we'll try out some of these phrases:

   "Thank you so much for asking, but I'm unable to do that."

   "I don't have the bandwidth for that, but I'm honored you asked."

   "I'm not available to make it. Thank you for asking!"

   "Thank you for thinking of me. I wish I were free, but I don't have the capacity right now."

   "I can't make it; thanks, though!"

   "I wish I could, but I can't do that at this time."

   "Please ask me again some other time. In this season that won't work for me."

OK, you've got what you need. If you're tired, and tired of being tired, there's no other way around this. So we are going to have to say no. But we can do it. Let's go.

The Ministry of Absence

Over ten years ago, Nick was pastoring at a church that we were helping to replant and recoup after a rough season. When we moved to that city, we had no idea what we were in for or what had been happening in that church. As soon as we got settled, it seemed like heartbreak after heartbreak showed up at our door.

The pastors were tired or just walking out. The people were bitter and frustrated. Families were struggling with massive trauma. There was beauty and grace but also a lot of heartache.

One night Nick's phone rang pretty late (for us), maybe 10:00 p.m., while he and I were sitting in bed reading. With all the church turmoil, Nick picked up, eager to see what was going on so late at night. I sat beside him, still, already praying, growing a little more anxious as he listened.

It was our new friend Sam, and he was pretty upset and flustered about something going on in his life. I won't give away all of his story, but I will say, it wasn't small, and I was shocked at what I heard Nick say in response.

"All right, man, if you're safe tonight, I'll get off the phone and pray for you. I want you to pray too. And why don't you come over tomorrow so we can talk?"

When he hung up, I questioned him. "Are you sure? This is pretty serious. Sam can come over tonight, or you can even go meet him! I don't want to leave him hanging."

Nick promised me that he was sure—but friends, I was dubious. Maybe even a little judgy. Nick was his pastor, and Sam was in pain! We needed to respond! We needed to help! Sam needed us!

I'll never forget what happened the next day.

Sam came over sometime midmorning and sat on the gold vintage sofa we'd inherited from my nana. The kids were playing upstairs—not even slightly quiet—but I made us some coffee, and we sat down to hear how he was doing.

"Well, it's kind of crazy," Sam started. "Last night, you told me to pray about it. And I did. And it was honestly the first time I ever prayed. For myself, for real. And now I think I'm a Christian. I felt God's presence and it worked. Last night changed my life."

I sat in disbelief. Nick wasn't smug—he's not a smug guy—but he wasn't even slightly surprised. Because he understood that the ministry of absence is a real thing. Sometimes we're so insistent on the importance of our presence that we forget about the presence of God. We believe the lie that we're holding these lives together with our bare hands, and we forget about the God who holds back the seas from the shore.

I love being a present person. I love serving, loving, leading, and being with people. I love saying yes when it's obedient. But I also love that my God works while I sleep. I love that my Father often gives better counsel than I ever could. I love that while my brain sees strategies and logistics, His holds the master plan that is full of miracles.

If you're tired because you're saying yes to everything and showing up in every space, it may be time to practice the ministry of absence. If you're exhausted because you've believed the lie that everything depends on you, it may be time to get a little more dependent on Jesus.

Maybe this means you let someone else put your kids to bed once in a while, knowing that your place in their life is more than established.

Maybe you skip girls' night on a busy week, knowing you'll be a more present friend for the long haul if you don't overextend yourself this week.

Practicing the ministry of absence could look like taking a season off from volunteering, leading, or organizing so you can find a more sustainable pace.

We won't be negligent or complacent, but we will pause and ask Holy Spirit to guide us before we say yes and show up in every space where there's a need. We won't ignore the needs of others, but we will remember that Jesus loves His kids more than we ever could. We won't hide or retreat from the callings He's given us. Still, we will ensure that we're sustaining a physical pace that agrees with the truth that we're daughters—not soldiers, not factory workers who can't quit, not housemaids who have to keep sweeping so no one notices that we've stopped.

We're daughters. The limitations of our physical bodies are not liabilities; rather, they're a gift from our Father so we can lean on Him and return to our belovedness. Let's slow down, listen to them, and fight the fatigue that plagues us.

Tips for Physical Low Power Mode

- Pause before saying yes to anything, no matter how simple it seems. Truly pray about the decision if you need to, and ask, *If I say yes to this, what is my reason for doing so?*
- Prioritize going to sleep well, not just waking up well (rest before work for your body).
- Normalize participation over performance. When you show up somewhere, pay attention to ways you may be trying to perform (your physical appearance, being early, being eager, trying to affect others' perception of you).
- Save your mental energy and rewrite the narrative when you talk about your physical limitations (your need for sleep, time off, quiet, etc.). Try not to apologize, explain, or talk negatively about your basic physical needs.

What Women Have to Say

"I just need to get through the next few weeks" was a constant broken promise to myself that I would reward my "perseverance" with a recommended amount of sleep. Healthy living became something I had to earn instead of a gift from God. But by the time I got to my promised sleep, I needed to stay up for myself because I had spent the day saying yes. Understanding that saying no, both to myself and others, could be considered holy changed my life. If the Holy Spirit wasn't saying yes, I said no. If I felt bad about getting an adequate amount of sleep because I wasn't being productive, I told myself no and gently explained that sleep—that rest—is productive.

Makayla, ministry leader and young wife

nine

mental exhaustion

"My brain is fried."[1]

The year 2020 was supposed to be our year. Maybe it was supposed to be your year too. Maybe you had declarations about moving ahead in work, spending more time in community, or finally sending your kids off to school. The heartbreak that came with the COVID-19 pandemic was extensive: the loss of life, mental health struggles, loss of community, and so much more. One grief for our family is that it was supposed to be our sabbatical year, and we'd saved and planned for years to do some extensive travel.

The idea of sabbatical comes from Leviticus 25, where God commands the Israelites to rest the land every seventh year. Interestingly, the practice wasn't applied to vocational jobs until 1880, when Harvard University initiated a sabbatical program for members of their faculty who were encouraged to take time off for study, leisure, and rest. By 1977, McDonald's was the first company to offer corporate sabbaticals for employees.[1]

I first heard about the concept of a sabbatical inside the church, an option offered to pastors after six years of work. If I'm being honest, however, it feels like a nice idea that is rarely executed. In fact, 72 percent of churches don't offer a sabbatical program.[2]

My unofficial data is this: I know a lot of pastors, and very few of them have taken a sabbatical.

Whether you're in ministry or not, the concept of resting the land seems incredibly important to me. When we work the land, it deserves to rest. When we work our bodies, our minds, our hearts, they deserve the rest.

Years before it came, 2020 was highlighted for Nick, and he told everyone we were going on a sabbatical. I'd ask many questions about how in the world we'd make it work, how we'd afford it, how the church would do without us, and how I could just stop working, writing, and traveling to teach. His insistence was always the same: We would figure it out, and God would provide because we needed to rest the land.

So, this was the plan: My dad lived in Bangkok then, so we would start there. Then, after that, we'd head to New Zealand, and we'd end our sabbatical with two weeks in Seattle—where we'd spent a handful of our early years as a family. We were going to leave behind laptops and prep the church for our departure, and I was going to take the entire time off from creating content or strategizing for our business in any way.

Of course, by March 2020, we knew our plans were probably changing as the global pandemic shut down one thing after another. By May, all our flights were refunded, and we were beginning to grieve the lack of a sabbatical, especially as learning how to pastor a local church through a pandemic had left us more exhausted than ever.

And then God made a way. There's a small private island near Charleston called Dewees Island. If you're conjuring images of a luxury getaway, stop right there. Dewees is private in that there are no cars, visitors, stores, or even roads on the island—just a handful of rustic houses, a small post office, and a dock for the ferry to bring people. We couldn't travel, but we could use some of our sabbatical money to rent a house for one month on this island where no one would be.

And so we did. We packed up the kids, our dog, a million books and journals, and enough sunscreen to sink the ferry and made our way to Dewees for July. What God did there in that month is a whole book in and of itself, but it's the first few days that I want to tell you about.

Those first few days were alarmingly quiet. There were no other people, tasks, social media, or projects to finish—just our family and an empty beach in front of our house. And I was . . . terrified. My brain was used to the stimulation. My soul was so used to the constant obligation, it felt like I didn't even know how to *think*. So I just worried about everything.

And then I read something so encouraging. I'd picked up Ruth Haley Barton's book *Invitation to Solitude and Silence*, and she warned that in the first few days of retreat or sabbatical, your brain will feel like a jar of dirt and water shaken aggressively. And when you stop everything suddenly and put the jar down, it takes time for the silt and soil to settle.[3]

All of our brains are overstimulated. The default setting for women in our current culture is overwhelmed, but that doesn't have to continue to be our reality. We don't have to keep consenting to live distracted, confused, and mentally exhausted.

Let Dr. Barton's metaphor be a helpful encouragement as we go: It will take time for the dust and dirt to settle, and it might even feel uncomfortable and overwhelming in our minds as we embrace biblical rest. Put another way, it might all feel worse before it starts to get better. But eventually, the soil settles and we can see clearly again.

Doesn't that sound worth it?

Jesus, Help

Traffic is heavy as I make my way from the coffee shop to work. I should be sad or scared that I will be a little late, but I'm mostly relieved for the mental reprieve. My friend and I had been rescheduling this coffee date for weeks and finally snuck it in before I had to be at the office, but I had no idea what I was in for when we met. She didn't say anything through text about how bad it had gotten with her husband—I'm not even sure she knows how bad it is—but now I can't stop thinking about how hard it is for anyone to make it in marriage.

At the stoplight, I plug in my phone (that I forgot to charge last night) and see that nine text messages have popped up since we started the coffee date. Two are work-related, two are spam for online sales, and five are from the group thread my extended family has—it seems there is a cousin who is in the hospital. I can't read all of them just yet. I'll look when I get to the office.

When the light turns green, I try desperately to clear my head and focus on the meeting I'm going to be late for while flashes of my friend are still popping up in my thoughts, and oh Lord, I just remembered that I didn't turn my curling wand off this morning. I know it has an automatic, fail-safe shutoff, but what if that fails? Another red light. I've just gone from being eight minutes late to twelve.

At this light, I open my phone to scroll for a second while I wait, something mind-numbing to ease the noise, and see two posts on social media that get embedded in my brain for the rest of the drive. The first is about the state of meat in the twenty-first century and how we're eating too much of it (somehow this problem I'm not even slightly qualified to solve feels like mine to turn over and over in my head). The second post I see is from the gal who leads my weekly Bible study. It was her birthday last weekend. I never texted her or bought a gift or a card, and now I'm wondering what in the world is wrong with me. I close social media; this isn't helping.

I open the Notes app to remind myself to tell her "happy birthday" and see the note I started during my commute last Thursday. I never got any of this figured out or finished. I'm about to pull into the office. My brain is fried. This isn't working. I'm doing my absolute best, and I still can't keep up.

"Jesus, help . . . ," I pray as I unbuckle my seat belt, grab my phone and bag, and hustle in late to the meeting.

Does any of this sound familiar? Jesus, help us!

This Music Is Too Loud

When I started struggling with the rolling panic attacks, mostly occurring at night, the days were tiring but the anxiety I felt during the day was mostly low-grade. I could work out. I could go to work. I could function. The wheels only truly came off at night. The panic attacks led to insomnia, one vicious cycle of horrible night after night.

It took a few months, visits with doctors and therapists, a ton of prayer, and mental health strategies—but relief came. I started sleeping again, and the nocturnal panic attacks came fewer and farther between.

Until Mexico.

Nick and I had gotten four nights at a resort in Mexico at a colossal discount they'd given for booking during the pandemic. The resort was obviously desperate to see money come in, so we'd purchased the stay and planned to use it later. In July of 2022, once I felt better and the time was right for our family, we snuck away to the resort for a little anniversary celebration and getaway.

I slept great at night and laughed and cuddled with my husband during the day, incredibly grateful for this tremendous gift of time and relaxation. And then it hit. One afternoon, we were just sitting by the pool, waiting on some tacos, listening to the poolside DJ, and feeling a bit older than all the young bucks bouncing around in the pool. Then, without warning, my chest started feeling tight, and I noticed my breaths were becoming shorter. I wasn't stressed, emotional, or actively worried about anything, yet my body was experiencing all the early signs of a panic attack.

I tried calming my mind and body without telling Nick I was struggling. But the music was so loud, the sun suddenly felt too

128

hot, and my body wasn't listening to my mind. Panic was rolling through all my limbs and streaming through my eyes in uncontrollable tears. I put my hand on Nick's arm, and when he looked at my face, he just knew and immediately sprang into action to help me. A few hours and a thousand tears later, I was back in our room, lying in bed, and trying to get my body to recover from what had happened. My nervous system was shot from hours of experiencing this trauma response, so I just lay still in the dark, hoping to fight the exhaustion I was feeling. I was trying not to be frustrated with myself, my brain, and my body for doing this to me on vacation; instead, I was trying to bless my body for reacting in defense in the face of overwhelming stimulation.

A few months later, after going panic-free for so long, I had another full-blown attack. This time, it was on a date with Nick at a new restaurant that had opened down the street from us. Cue the exact same experience: panic, tears, recovery, exhaustion. When I compared the two occasions and tried to search for what might have been the catalyst, I knew in my gut that the common denominator in both situations was the loud music.

A quick Google search asking, "Does loud music cause panic attacks?" will make you pretty confident you have a rare condition called "phonophobia" (at least it did for me). Ultimately, I don't think the noise itself caused the panic, but I do believe that the overstimulation caused my brain to reach a point of overextension.

And this is the thing: I refuse to believe that my brain and body are broken because they can't handle constant provocation. Simply put, we are not the problem because we can't handle constant mental exertion in every setting, all day. None of us are meant to.

And what does this have to do with exhaustion? We were given five senses to experience the world to the glory of God: sight, smell, sound, taste, and touch. But for most of us, our current cultural settings have turned up the volume on every single sensation to the point where we are all experiencing almost constant sensory overload. As our brains and bodies are busy processing this stimulation, they require energy, which causes exertion that is nearly undetectable to us and leaves us feeling tired.

Much of your mental exhaustion has nothing to do with your capacity, strength, toughness, or even your life choices. Our culture has largely robbed us of quiet, undistracted, boring, and unprovoked moments. This doesn't mean we don't have hope. It does mean we'll have to go back to basics and reclaim some margin for our minds.

There's a reason why Psalm 23 tells us that our Father wants to lead us to still waters and makes us lie down in open pastures. There's a reason why David wrote so many psalms alone in caves while he cried out to God. There's a reason why Jesus had to escape the crowds, whom He had come to love, save, and serve, to get time alone with God. There's a reason why Moses heard best from God on the mountain, not surrounded by the Israelites barking at him.

I love technology; I love feeling connected to the world around me—the life, color, events, and noise. And I've already told you I like to watch TV in the shower. But I cannot fight mental exhaustion adequately when I don't have regulated and rhythmic moments without provocation. And neither can you. Overstimulation is exhausting us mentally, but it's also taking a toll on our bodies and souls in a lasting way.

Multitasking Is a Myth

For years, I prided myself on my capacity to do ten things at once until I realized I was just doing them all less focused than I could have been. Dr. Caroline Leaf is the first person I ever heard denounce multitasking in a way that makes sense to me. Here's what she shares:

> The truth about multitasking is that it is a persistent myth. What we really do is shift our attention rapidly from task to task, resulting

in two bad things: (1) We don't devote as much focused attention as we should to a specific activity, task, or piece of information, and (2) we sacrifice the quality of our attention. . . .

This poor focusing of attention and lack of quality in our thought lives is the complete opposite of how the brain is designed to function and causes a level of brain damage. Every rapid, incomplete, and poor quality shift of thought is like making a milkshake with your brain cells and neurochemicals.[4]

What if your mental exhaustion is less about a lack of energy and more about a consistent state of divided attention? It's wild to me how I also see this scientific principle mirrored in the simplicity of Scripture.

Proverbs 4:25 tells us, "Let your eyes look straight ahead; fix your gaze directly before you."

Hebrews 3:1 reminds us to "fix your thoughts on Jesus, whom we acknowledge as our apostle and high priest."

Philippians 3:13–14 says, "But one thing I do: Forgetting what is behind and straining toward what is ahead, I press on toward the goal to win the prize for which God has called me heavenward in Christ Jesus."

To fight multitasking in a kingdom-minded way, we don't have to sit in a room and think solely about Jesus all day. But we will have to work to clarify our purposes on a macro and micro level so we don't live with a divided and exhausted mind.

That's Not Mine to Carry

I was born without a filter, specifically over my mouth. So if something is true or feels true, my brain lacks the innate capacity to do anything but say it. The great news is that you'll always know where you stand with me. The bad news is that sometimes I say too much, exposing either my soul or other people with my onslaught of honesty.

By the power of the Holy Spirit and the mercy of social cues, I've grown a filter—just a small one. And I'm learning that I don't have to share the whole truth, nothing but the truth, with every single person, all the time. So, when someone asks how I'm doing on a Sunday morning at church, I don't have to give the fake party line of "Good. Busy, but good!" (unless that's true). And at the same time, I don't have to answer with the entirely too honest, "I'm a little gassy, fighting some comparison with my sister, anxious about how this service will go down, but overall feeling pretty OK!"

Thus, when anyone has asked me the specifics about my exhaustion/anxiety breakdown-that-was-really-a-breakthrough, I do the quick mental dance in my head to figure out how much is safe to share. Do you know that dance? Where you want to be transparent and honest, but you also don't want to tell them so much that they wish they hadn't asked? I've learned to give my answer in phases to adequately assess when and where to stop sharing, either because the listener has lost interest or because we're not close enough for me to let them in on my most intimate stories.

Here's how it goes:

Curious Acquaintance: "Hey! I remember you were struggling with anxiety and insomnia last year. How is that going? Are you doing OK?"

Me: "Thanks so much for asking. I'm feeling a lot better." (Pause for assessment and see if they ask another question.)

Curious Acquaintance: "Wow, I'm so glad to hear it. I know you were asking for prayer a lot; it seemed intense. What do you feel helped you get out of it?"

Me: "I mean, for sure, God, but He led me to use many different strategies. I saw two different doctors and a spiritual director. I had to start practicing sleep hygiene. I had to step back from my role at church. The medicine helped, journaling helped, but ultimately—I had a lot of soul work to do." (Pause for assessment. If they ask one more question, this is typically my favorite part of the conversation—because I get to share what I'm about to share with you.)

Curious Acquaintance: "Do you have any idea what caused it or brought the struggle on?"

Me: "To be honest, yeah. After a lot of processing and prayer, I'm pretty sure this had been building for years. Maybe longer. At my core, I was wrestling with over-responsibility. I thought everything around me was mine to hold. I couldn't rest because I couldn't stop living like I had to solve it all, fix it all, and sort everything out all the time. And the real problem is that once you start believing this lie, you're often rewarded for it. Over time, I thought everything was mine to hold and I forgot God holds it all."

Curious Acquaintance: "OK, wow, that's more than I thought you'd share—but I'm glad to hear it."

Our culture expects, encourages, and rewards women for working from a place of over-responsibility. It starts when you take a little more onto your mental plate, probably motivated by love or devotion to God. The problem a friend is going through, the family you read about on social media who is experiencing tragedy, the systemic problem that's burdening so many. The snack schedule that's not working in your kid's class, your mom's frustration with your dad the last time you visited, the coworker who refuses to get that lump checked out. The temptation to figuratively pick up the burdens around us is somehow both involuntary and, by nature, voluntary at once.

Just as we're continually tempted to push past our physical boundaries needed for rest, the same is true for our mental load.

In fact, it's actually harder to identify our limits when they're so internal and even more difficult to communicate to others when we've hit the edge of what we can possibly *think* about.

But if we don't, we'll be unable to catch our mental breath because the crushing weight of every concern will be swirling in our brains. How do we process this? How do we care for other people without carrying their burdens?

I'm encouraged by so many stories from the life of Jesus just to remember that it's possible for us to love others sincerely and also not believe that it's our actual duty to meet their every need.

I think about when Lazarus died in John 11. It was clear that Jesus loved His friend and would mourn him—but He still waited two days to see him after hearing he was sick.

I think about Luke 22, just before Jesus's death, when He left to pray. If I'm honest, if I put myself in Jesus's shoes with my imagination, nine times out of ten I imagine I'd be getting in all my last words with the disciples or preparing everyone else for what was ahead.

It's estimated that there are forty-one counts of Jesus walking away from the people He loved, for one reason or another, in the Gospels. Forty-one times that He withdrew, got alone, said no, or just did not stay—even when the entire purpose of His coming to earth was to seek and save these people.

I can't take from this that Jesus is some overly boundaried, unkind, unfeeling, and cold person. The entire gospel tells me differently. So instead, I have to read between the lines to learn a whole new truth, one that isn't preached to most women.

It is entirely possible to care for people without assuming that every one of their burdens is ours to carry. And that applies to the mental load we accept and believe to be ours for the taking.

As I've been writing this book, I've had a handful of very close friends walking through some incredibly traumatic experiences. As I've sought to be on their team and show up for them, one of the biggest struggles has been finding mental autonomy. When

I'm not with them, I often instinctively feel guilty for not thinking about them. Or when I am with them, I find myself working under the assumption that it's my responsibility to give them the best advice and fix every single one of their problems.

Here's what's most interesting: If I took this assumption as truth and believed that loving my friends equated to fixing all their problems and thinking about them constantly, I'd actually have two issues. The first is that I'd be completely mentally exhausted and potentially unable to cope with my own life. The second is that, ultimately, my friends might feel not like they are loved but like they're just projects for me to fix, problems for me to solve. And for every moment I would try to use my own mental energy to bring healing in their lives, they may eventually wish I'd just sit with them and hold space for their grief.

This doesn't even account for the crushing weight of mental tension that comes from being an overly connected and communicative society. Fifty years ago, our grandparents didn't have the option to know what was happening politically, socially, relationally, and financially in every place at all times. I don't hate technology and don't want to bury my head in the sand, but I do realize the enormous toll that access to information takes on our brains. Most of us cannot possibly sort out what is ours to hold and what is not when culture tells us we must keep up with everything all at once.

Codependency is an emotional and behavioral condition that affects someone's capacity to have a healthy, functioning relationship. The problem of codependency revolves around the issue of *enmeshment*, a word used to describe what happens when a person loses touch with where their identity begins and ends in regard to other people. When an individual becomes so intertwined with one or more people, they begin to lose their sense of self, their autonomy. Codependency manifests itself in many ways that span the spectrum, ranging from feeling responsible for solving other people's problems to valuing other people's opinions more than you value your own.

Codependency is developed from a myriad of issues, such as growing up neglected or overprotected, trauma, divorce, and most certainly any kind of abuse. This all makes sense when you consider that in these environments, the boundary lines between one human and another are intensely blurred to the point of confusing enmeshment.

I share all of this to make two points: First, if you think you may struggle with codependency, I'd like to encourage you by saying that it's not your fault and there is help. Your brain and behavior developed around and in response to the struggles you faced, but your brain can grow new neuropathways, and you can learn new and healthy behavior. This might be a great moment to find a trauma-informed therapist or do a little side reading on codependency from a professional perspective. I'll share a few of my favorite resources in the back of this book.

I'd imagine that for many of us, some level of codependency has snuck into our relationships, leading to physical and spiritual exhaustion. But our thought life is the base layer where we can set boundaries and regain autonomy. You are your own God-imagined person with thoughts, opinions, stories, and outlooks all your own. If you're mentally exhausted because you're constantly thinking about the problems, well-being, and approval of others, I believe there's a lot of freedom available for you. I believe there's rest available for you. In the next chapter, we're going to talk about how we can practically care for others without trying to carry them, but for now I want you to get your hopes up. Maybe there's a lot of work to be done here, perhaps this is an area where you need a lot of healing, but that means there is a lot of relief ahead. Seeing the problem means there is hope for the solution. Let's keep going.

Only Volunteers

I think there's a quote from *The West Wing* for almost every problem. And so, as we're talking about the issue of distraction, I'm going to cut straight to one of my favorites.

In one episode, when Sam (the deputy speech writer) is getting riled up about a tell-all book that's about to be published about the White House, C.J. Cregg (the White House communications director) says this: "Let me tell you something I've learned in my years. There are victims of fires. There are victims of car accidents. This kind of thing, there are no victims—just volunteers."[5] C.J. is suggesting that Sam was volunteering to get riled up about something he couldn't control. I think that we often volunteer to be distracted. At the very least we continually consent.

I remember the first time I saw that episode (you don't want to know how many times I've seen it since). I almost spit out the coffee I was drinking.

There are parts of exhaustion that I can't escape in this life. I can't personally do much but hold on and respond as healthily as possible. But there are parts of my exhaustion, specifically my mental exhaustion, that I volunteer for. And one of those is allowing myself to live constantly distracted.

Working distracted makes us less effective, driving distracted makes us dangerous, trying to love others while we're distracted leaves us frustrated with ourselves. Our minds and souls are suffering because we've become so accustomed to having one million tabs open in our brains.

Again, we'll get into the practicals of correcting this in the next chapter, but for now, let's hold our part in this onslaught of brain fatigue. So much of our tiredness is due to the effects of living in a broken and fallen world. But so much of it is because we're allowing ourselves to constantly be pushed and pulled mentally.

Our brains are tired because they're overstimulated, forced to multitask when they weren't made for it, holding more problems and tensions than they were created for, and constantly facing distraction from what matters. We didn't start this fight, and we didn't cause these problems, but we don't have to continually consent to them.

The question once again is this: Are we tired enough of being tired? Would we rather keep going the way we are right now, or would we rather stop living with fried brains? I believe there's so much hope ahead for us. And more than that, I believe there is deep peace that passes worldly understanding if we'll press in.

Reflection Questions

1. Metaphorically speaking, how's the dirt in your jar? Swirling or starting to settle?
2. What factors lead you to feel overstimulated?
3. How often do you multitask, and is it serving you?
4. Have you experienced the difference between caring and carrying?

Symptoms of Mental Exhaustion in Our Lives

- Stress headaches
- Trouble sleeping
- Feeling confused or behind
- Numbing out
- Poor memory or cognitive function
- Feeling panicked or anxious

Verses to Meditate On

2 Timothy 1:7

For God has not given us a spirit of fear, but of power and of love and of a *sound mind*. (NKJV, emphasis added)

Psalm 34:17

The righteous cry out, and the LORD hears them;
he delivers them from all their troubles.

2 Corinthians 1:3-4

Praise be to the God and Father of our Lord Jesus Christ, the Father of compassion and the God of all comfort, who comforts us in all our troubles, so that we can comfort those in any trouble with the comfort we ourselves receive from God.

ten

mental exhaustion

"Peace is my birthright."

I have very few Bible verses memorized. I have the concepts of a lot of Scripture in my heart and can give a passing paraphrase when needed, but I'm not great at reciting word for word.

Isaiah 26:3 is one of the exceptions.

I say it in parts as a breath prayer, a promise I can recite from God's heart to mine.

It looks something like this for me:

Deep breath in: "You keep her . . ."
Deep breath out: "in perfect peace . . ."
Deep breath in: "whose mind . . ."
Deep breath out: "is stayed on You . . ."
Deep breath in: "because she trusts in You."[1]
Deep breath out: "Amen."

When my husband was in the hospital with heart problems, when my kid was struggling with depression, when I'm waiting on a response to a tense email, when the car is on empty and I'm five miles from a gas station.

Whether it's a big and scary situation or just everyday stress, I go back to this promise from our Father: He will keep us in perfect peace when we keep our minds on Him.

I've learned over time that living in perfect peace isn't always feeling perfectly peaceful. But the supernatural effect of knowing the God who made you, loves you, holds you, and cares more for your life than you ever could does bring a comfort that is beyond our comprehension.

Maybe we've forgotten who we are.

It's almost always an identity issue. I can almost laugh now, thinking about how so many of our spiritual struggles and strongholds are rooted in a misunderstanding of our identity.

You're feeling insecure—that's an identity issue. We forget that we're daughters of the Most High God, loved and set apart for His glory.

You're angry and bitter at people in your community—kind of an identity issue. We forget how much we've been forgiven, we forget our identity is rooted in receiving lavish grace, and we stop forgiving others.

You're struggling to make a decision—identity! We forget that we're His kids who get to ask Him for insight whenever we need something and that we get to ask without wavering in doubt that He'll respond.

And it will take adjusting our understanding of our kingdom identity to break free from mental exhaustion. Here's why: Peace that passes understanding is our birthright as sons and daughters of God. It's His promise to those of us who keep our minds stayed on His goodness. And it's a promise we can take Him up on as much as we need to.

Mental peace was purchased on our behalf with the body and blood of our Savior. It is ours for the taking, for the claiming, but doing so will mean breaking up with the busy-glorifying culture that tells us strong women carry it all, push through at all costs, and are accessible at all times.

Embracing the peace that is ours will mean putting down the labels that we were never meant to come into agreement with:

"I'm a mess."

"I've got mom brain."

"I'm a nervous wreck."

"I'm so stupid."

"I can't think straight."

"My brain is fried."

Before we can embrace the practices that will help us fight the mental fatigue we're facing, the most fruitful thing we can do is come into alignment with what is true about us. Our brains were made good by a Father who loves us and wants wholeness for us. Our minds have been given the capacity to interact with the Spirit that brought love back to life. And our Friend and Savior said this to His friends just before His death ushered in our resurrection:

> Peace I leave with you; my peace I give you. I do not give to you as the world gives. Do not let your hearts be troubled and do not be afraid. (John 14:27)

These words of Jesus, spoken between the Last Supper and the garden of Gethsemane, aren't insignificant to our identity. These words aren't just about what He was giving those in His midst but about what we have access to while we live under the effects of this fallen and broken world.

This is our inheritance. Peace is our birthright in the family of God. We weren't made for discombobulated, scrambled, and constantly confused living. So what gives, and why aren't we operating out of this wholeness of mind that is ours for the taking?

We Need a Third Way

I find there are two predominantly popular perspectives regarding our mental state within the church. Unfortunately, I don't find either to be all that comprehensive or helpful, though I can still appreciate the heart behind how people got to these perspectives.

Let's call the first way "spiritual denial." Out of love and honor for God, many Christians have believed that mental health struggles (as well as many physical health struggles) were defeated on the cross of Christ, and the resurrection purchased our complete and immediate physical healing. What I believe about people who engage in spiritual denial is this: They mean to glorify God, but the intent and the impact are often not the same.

The theological question of why and when God heals here on earth—and when He doesn't—is a complex one. It was a complex one even for Jesus, who left people unhealed as He ministered and answered tough questions about why they were wounded in the first place. So, as we keep a firm grasp on our reverence and honor for God and the belief that He can heal anything and loves His kids deeply, we can take a step back to see that sometimes He still allows physical (and mental) struggles here on earth. In fact, He reminds us in His Word that His power is often displayed best in our places of weakness.

The implications of this theology trickle down and impact a myriad of areas in our lives. Still, I want to highlight one effect, specifically concerning our mental exhaustion. This spiritual denial often manifests itself in the refusal to acknowledge the effects this fallen world has on our brain, specifically in the form of anxiety, worry, fear, and confusion.

Spiritual denial says there is no space for struggle where faith is found. Spiritual denial says that we won't be scared or concerned if we trust God enough. And yet, again, a more zoomed-out picture will often show us that the faith and belief we hold fast to in the midst of our brokenness, anxiety, and confusion are more steadfast than we could ever imagine.

Simply put, when I see women trust God in the midst of their mental fatigue and affliction, I am so inspired and encouraged by the wild faith it takes to trust for His ultimate healing while they still live under the effects of this fallen world. Denying the existence of our mental fatigue and its impact is not spiritual maturity; rather, it's denying one of the spaces in which we can see God move.

Often when we realize how serious the effects of spiritual denial are, we pendulum-swing to another belief system that is also rooted in great love but leaves us wanting more. Let's call this way "earthly agreement." In this case—again, often motivated by a deep compassion for others (and ourselves)—we see a total acceptance of the experiences of earth as our new and complete identity.

Instead of experiencing anxiety as a condition, we let the condition speak for the fullness of our identity and agree with the label that we are anxious people. Instead of experiencing the effects of sickness and brokenness in this world, we accept the labels of our illnesses and personalities, identifying more with our temporal diagnoses than our spiritual inheritance.

An example of this would be saying "I am an anxious person" instead of "I am experiencing anxiety." Or "I'm a nervous wreck" instead of "This week has been really hectic, and I'm taking it day by day." It might sound like semantics or like we're trying to trick ourselves into believing something, but honestly, the words we speak about ourselves become the words we believe about ourselves.

We need a third way. Our lives are not black and white, our struggles are not black and white, and a colorful and vibrant life requires more than proclamations of just "good" or "bad," "anxious" or "full of faith." More than one thing can be true in the kingdom.

We need compassion for how our brains and bodies are exposed to brokenness here on earth because our Savior is undoubtedly coming toward us with mercy and kindness. And we also need a firm understanding of our intact spiritual identity amid mental exhaustion.

We are women who feel stress and are more than conquerors in Christ Jesus.

We are women who experience anxiety, and peace is also our birthright.

We are women who know what it means to worry about those we love, and we can feel anxious even as we profess Christ as King.

We don't pretend that the problems of this world don't exist, and we don't abandon our kingdom identity either.

This identity agreement is so wildly crucial because these small shifts we will make for our mental exhaustion (not letting our anxiety define us) will mean nothing if they're not rooted in a more significant shift of understanding who we are in Christ Jesus. Simply put, having a firm foundation of kingdom truth regarding who God is and who He says we are will help us when it's time to practically speak truth in our everyday lives.

Peace is our birthright, but I don't believe our Father would have promised us peace that passes all understanding if He pretended that our struggle wasn't real. Amen?

Silence and Solitude

Do you know when a kid (or an immature adult) begrudgingly shows you something they want to hide from you? Maybe they drag their feet as they make their way to you, avert their eyes when they hand it over, or make an actual growling noise as they sullenly supply whatever it is you asked for?

This is what my kids look like when they don't want to show me their report cards (joke's on them; the school emailed them to me already—I just want to see them hand them over) or my dog when I make him drop the small dead animal he found in the backyard. Or . . . just how I look when it's time to review the monthly credit card report with my husband.

It's also how I want you to picture me now as I tell you this: There's no way you and I can fight mental exhaustion without embracing some practice of silence and solitude.

I set out to write a book for real women, not just the ones who can afford silent retreats and sound baths. I set out to write a book to help us embrace practices of realistic rest for the sake of our souls, bodies, and minds.

But no matter which way I turn, how much research I do, or how begrudgingly I offer this information, the facts are facts: We cannot fight mental fatigue—specifically overstimulation—without silence and solitude. It's often in the quiet moments of silence and solitude where we learn and absorb the everyday truths that will help us when life is loud and overwhelming.

Now here's the GREAT news: Silence and solitude are free. And they're accessible, even if we have to fight for them, at the very least in small slivers, in every season.

I'll still be a gal who enjoys people, noise, and action. I still listen to the same loud worship album during every book I write (John Mark McMillan, *Live at the Knight*), and I can still fill almost any void in conversation with a couple of quick words.

But I have also (begrudgingly) come to appreciate, respect, and even love realistic practices of silence and solitude. I now routinely take small moments to embrace silence on a daily basis because there is no getting around the truth that it helps me connect better with God and myself.

For years, I've traveled to teach the Bible and coach women, and for years, I've brought someone with me on every trip (my husband, a kid, an assistant, or a friend) because I hate being alone. Until a few years ago when a series of strange events left me in Wisconsin for a three-day work trip with no support person and only one speaking event to attend during that time.

I panicked when I got dropped off at the hotel and realized I'd be largely alone for the next few days. I let the waves of anxiety hit my body, and then I audibly said, "OK, God—what do You want to do?" Over the next seventy-two hours, I was overwhelmed to find that once the shock and fear wore off, I sensed the presence of God in ways I never had before. I could hear myself think, I could sort out complex emotions that I'd been shelving for months, and I was getting wild vision for my calling and business.

I wasn't just experiencing the void of community or a lack of noise. I was experiencing the loudness of God in silence and solitude.

Maybe you love being alone; maybe it's your all-too-often reality and you can't relate to my reluctance. Or maybe you're not as terrified of the quiet as I am, but you realize you still often fill the silence with something.

I think it's interesting that for many of us, there is genuine fear found at the root of keeping our lives noisy and overstimulating. We're scared of what we'll find to be true about God, scared of what we'll find to be true about us, or just plain afraid to stop.

But I'm here to report, as a silence and solitude convert, that embracing practices of quiet—when we're in a place to do so healthily—will not only help us fight mental fatigue, it'll help us uncover the wonder and mystery of God in ways we never anticipated. It's OK to be scared, but it's not OK to keep turning up the noise in your life and turning down the sacred invitation to the presence of God.

Something important to note here, however, is that we're not always in seasons where silence and solitude are the healthiest for us. If you're in a season of battling anxiety or depression, where drawing inward or being alone is harmful, there is no shame in saving this practice for a time when it will be life-giving to do so. Your safety and wellness come first, and I believe our Father would wholeheartedly agree. In this case, getting professional help or spending time in safe community where you can process your struggles should be the first priority.

Thankfully, we can ask God for wisdom about what is best for us and listen to Holy Spirit's prompting to know whether this is a season for activating silence and solitude regularly. If and when it feels like a practice for you, here are a few ideas for starting a realistic practice of silence and solitude:

- Turn off the podcasts and music when you're alone in the car. Instead, start your time with a prayer inviting God to speak.

- Remove your phone from your bedroom and get an old-school alarm. Then put your phone to bed well before bedtime to embrace some quiet time in your brain, and don't pick it up till you've experienced some quiet in the morning.

- When on a girls' trip or couples' getaway, propose the idea of a few quiet hours. For staff/women's retreats and even trips with Nick, we like to do this the last morning we're away—a few hours of being silent together.

- Use headphones while grocery shopping, doing chores around the house, or exercising. Keep it on noise-canceling or play quiet instrumental music.

- Set up Do Not Disturb or time limits on your phone. Use them.

- Embrace the magic of sitting in your car before you go inside your house, but instead of scrolling on your phone—take a moment of silence.

- Take a screen-free night once a week as a family or by yourself.

- Get in the habit of leaving your phone behind for small moments as often as possible: to go on a short walk, when you take the kids to the park, when you walk around the mall, when you go into church, or when you eat out at a restaurant. You'll be shocked at how many moments of silence and solitude crop up when you're phone free. (Bonus: Being without our phones helps fight the codependent feeling that we must always be available to everyone.)

Let Passion Get Loud

When it comes to rest and fighting exhaustion, I like to err on the side of adding in rather than taking away. This is just my personality and how I see the kingdom of God: more as one of addition, making our lives more whole, than one of subtraction.

So, while silence and solitude look like subtraction, I honestly believe they are an addition: making space for the power and presence of God.

In the same way, our next practice for fighting mental exhaustion is all about addition. Let's add passionate focus to our lives. In the last chapter, we talked about the myth of multitasking and its negative effect on our lives. But what if our efforts to fight multitasking were more centered on increasing our passionate focus on what matters?

I love the CEB version of Romans 12:11: "Don't hesitate to be enthusiastic—be on fire in the Spirit as you serve the Lord!"

The best way we can fight the urge to multitask is by unleashing our attention on what matters and allowing ourselves to access the passion behind whatever we currently have our hands to. When we remove the culturally appropriate lids of our God-given passions, resisting the temptation to multitask is much easier.

One thing that keeps us from going all in on our passion and purpose is the cultural expectation that we, as women, should not be too much—you know, we should be pretty chill and easygoing, tempering our excitement and enthusiasm. But what if that zeal and devotion are a gift from God to help us be fully present and awake to the mental task in front of us?

What if you made space for wild passion to produce focus in you—whether it was in your work, your family, your community, your home, your project, your exercise, or even your rest? What would happen if you fought the fear that keeps you from going all in on what matters to you and instead risked it all by zeroing in on wherever you find yourself at the moment? Is it possible that stripping away all the secondary things might make even more capacity and passion for what really matters? In this way, is it possible that less really is more?

One of my favorite catchphrases (and the title of a previous book I wrote) is "take it too far." When it comes to your mental exhaustion, the call is not to tone down your passion but to *focus* your passion where your purpose is found. Just let your passion increase your purpose in the pursuit you find yourself in at the moment. Let's fight multitasking with massive zeal and see if it's not more manageable for our brains to process, heal, and move forward.

Here are some ideas for practicing passionate focus:

- Before you move into your day, review your schedule with God and meditate on why it matters.
- Ask God to help you see others—your roommates, coworkers, kids, or the people you serve at work—as He sees them.
- Write mini purpose statements for areas of your life that sometimes distract you from your God-given purpose, no matter how healthy they are (e.g., social media, hobbies, communities, etc.).
- Set timers to work on small projects or create reward systems to encourage a singular focus on tasks. Examples: "I'm taking twenty minutes to cuddle with my kiddo undistracted"; "I'm putting down my phone for two hours to read this book outside"; and "After I write two thousand words of this book—I'll make a fun cup of coffee."

Bottom line: Don't turn down the passion to turn up the focus in your life. We'll find so much mental health and rest when we go fully forward in singular focus in the areas where we can, when we're able.

Leave It at the Taco Shop

"Let's leave it at the taco shop," Nick said. He was standing at the front door, our dog leashed up and ready to go. It was a Friday, and we were trying as hard as possible to practice the Sabbath. Well, Nick was trying. I was resisting.

About a half mile from our house, there's a little corner store called Torres Superettes. If you drive by it, you can easily miss it.

There are bars on the window and weathered signs alerting you that you can buy lottery tickets there. But inside Torres Superettes are the world's best tacos, made by a small family we've come to love. My favorite taco is the al pastor, but my kids go for the beef or the chicken.

The tacos are world-class, authentic, and just purely delicious. And there's nothing better than a walk to the taco shop on a warm Charleston day, which is why Nick decided that's where we should leave our problems.

On Fridays, which were our joint Sabbath for that season of life, we'd spend the walk to Torres Superettes being honest about what was crowding our minds. So Nick made up this little game, "leaving it at the taco shop." The "it" was any mental struggle stealing my peace on the Sabbath. Sometimes it was an issue at work or church. Sometimes it was a fear about one of our kids, sometimes an argument or tension with a friend, and sometimes a gnawing sense of defeat or dread.

On the walk there, we'd air our concerns. Then, once we started the walk back, we'd both promise to let our minds move on to something else if the concern resurfaced.

John Eldredge calls this "benevolent detachment" in his book *Get Your Life Back*. Here's what he says about the practice:

> Mature adults have learned how to create a healthy distance between themselves and the thing they have become entangled with. Thus the word "detachment." It means getting untangled, stepping out of the quagmire; it means peeling apart the Velcro by which this person, relationship, crisis, or global issue has attached itself to you. Or you to it. Detachment means getting some healthy distance. Social media overloads our empathy. So I use the word "benevolent" in referring to this necessary kind of detachment because we're not talking about cynicism or resignation. Benevolent means kindness. It means something done in love. Jesus invites us into a way of living where we are genuinely comfortable turning things over to him.[2]

In a practical sense, Nick and I use a prayer we also heard from John Eldredge to live this out well: "Father, I release everyone and everything to You."[3]

When the thought comes, when the worry presents itself, when I am tempted to believe that I am responsible for the well-being, health, wholeness, and happiness of all the people in my life, I say, "Father, I release everyone and everything to You."

The physical act of saying this prayer (often out loud) helps my heart come into agreement with the very good news that I am not God. I cannot love people as well as He can. I cannot fix all their problems. I cannot meet all their needs. They will often not be served by me thinking about their issues, and to be completely honest, I'm rarely served by worrying or stressing about my own issues.

Ways to practice benevolent detachment:

- Find your own taco shop. Pick a place you can go, preferably close by, where you can figuratively leave your mental stress when it's time to rest.
- Write longer than normal, releasing prayers for particularly worrisome or essential issues. For example, when one of my kids struggles, I write and recite a prayer that helps me access the intimacy of asking God for relief while also surrendering to my powerlessness.
- Use brain dumps as prayer lists. For example, when my mind feels overloaded with issues, I'll list everything that burdens me and then pray over the entire list—offering it to God for His help.
- For particularly problematic concerns, I'll journal and ask three questions:
  1. Has God asked me to handle this problem?
  2. What can I do to help?
  3. What promises of God can I claim while I wait for Him to truly bring relief?

Practicing Presence

We're all prone to distraction, and it's easy for us to get caught up in it. When we're talking to our kids, our phones are dinging nearby. When we're supposed to be working on an important project, a million menial tasks threaten to steal our focus. When we spend time with God, forget about it—anything can derail us from practicing being present with our Father. The struggle is real for all of us.

Did you know it's actually scientifically impossible to live entirely in the present? Because our brains are constantly processing the sights, sounds, smells, and feelings of the second or millisecond we just lived, we're always living in the past. We're constantly distracted from the present. So, grace to you if you're not absolutely obsessed with living in the present. If your natural state isn't smelling every flower or enjoying the sensation of a spring rain hitting your skin, you're in a safe place.

Most of us gravitate to either the future or the past, imagining or replaying one or the other. But paying attention in the present doesn't come as naturally for various reasons.

I've learned three tactics that help me practice being present in a way that leaves my mind feeling more at ease, rested, and less like I just missed whatever was happening:

1. Notice
2. Say thanks
3. Accept how it is

Whether it's a quick check-in with my heart early in the morning, a family vacation, a stressful meeting at work, or a worshipful encounter at a women's conference, I want to live in the present and practice being fully awake right where I'm at. I'm assuming you do too. So, this is how we'll spend less energy processing what took place and conserve strength and vitality for what's to come.

1. *Notice what's happening.* Engage all five senses, capture, pay attention, and enjoy. How does that stack of papers feel in your hand during the meeting? What does that dinner you're cooking smell like? What colors do you notice on the walk with your friend? How does the ground feel beneath your feet as you stand to worship in church? What does your toddler's laugh sound like as you tickle them before bed?

   You can stay in the moment when you notice the moment. But to engage your mind meaningfully, take this further than literally. Notice how you feel, where your mind is wandering when it wanders, how the space you're in feels spiritually, and what seems to be happening underneath the surface.

2. *Say thanks, and express gratitude.* To keep our minds practicing our own presence and the presence of God, we can live out Psalm 16:6 and declare that the boundary lines have fallen in pleasant places for us. Think of things you're grateful for and keep a list of them on your phone, list them in your head in prayer, or say them out loud to a friend.

3. *Accept how it is.* One reason our brains fight so hard to ruminate in the past or skip ahead to the future and then end up exhausted is that we don't often love what we're experiencing in the present. Instead, we wish it was how it used to be, or we hope it will shift into something else in the future.

   But one way we can take some mental energy back is to accept how things are in the moment, knowing that God's power is made perfect in weakness and the miraculous is often found in the mundane.

I'm so grateful that we have a Father who is compassionate about our mental fatigue and offers us simple and supernatural ways forward from this fatigue.

Agree that peace is our birthright.

Embrace moments of silence and solitude.

Choose passionate focus on what matters in our lives.

Benevolently detach from believing every problem is ours to solve.

And practice being present in our own lives.

Fighting mental exhaustion is not *always* that simple, but often it is. Let's do the simple and small things we can do to bring rest and peace to our minds.

Tips for Mental Low Power Mode

- Utilize brain dumps (one minute of writing down everything on your mind) to clarify what is clogging your energy.
- Set timers to focus on or finish tasks, and play around with rewards to create brain satisfaction when you're done.
- Assign days or times to tasks, concerns, or responsibilities so that you don't live like you must do everything all at once.
- Take social media and/or news media breaks when needed.
- Turn on read receipts for emails and text messages; open them only when you have time and margin to respond.
- Normalize taking longer to make decisions.
- Block sites or apps that you find distracting so you can break the innate urge to open or visit those pages.

What Women Have to Say

Sometimes I feel like my mind is truly on overdrive and I cannot get it to stop. Figuring out schedules, planning all the things, making sure I don't miss opportunities, and trying to meet everyone's needs can be exhausting. Then adding in the often-too-much time I spend on social media, my mind does not get a break. Jess's practical tools have helped me turn down the noise of life so the voice of God can get louder. His voice speaks peace. His voice draws me to true places of rest and renewal. As I "fix my gaze on Him," I am able to home in on the most important things, turn things over to Him that I am not called to do, and rest in the assurance of who He is and what He can do.

Lanessa, 43, pastor, pastor's wife, and momma

eleven

emotional exhaustion

"I can't even."

That I can recall, I've been seriously involved in nine different churches. I'll keep it real with you: I've never been casually involved at any church. I'm an all-or-nothing kind of gal, so at all nine of those, I've been pretty intimately aware of the leadership structure and what it looks like for a follower of Jesus to flourish in that church setting.

I'm sad to say, but of those nine, only maybe two or three have made space for the way God works in and through our emotions to lead as we mature spiritually. I'm also sad to say that at least two or three negated the importance of our feelings in a potentially toxic way.

We landed at one such church just as I was freshly healing from severe postpartum depression, probably for the second time. I say "probably" because the first time I expressed intensely sad feelings after having a baby, no one in my immediate community had the language or capacity to acknowledge what I was dealing with. The few times I got courageous enough to say, "I think I'm struggling with postpartum," I was told that I was probably just tired or that it was my hormones talking.

I'm not angry or bitter at the people in my life who shut down those admissions. We were all doing the best we could at the time. And at that time, very few Christians had language that compassionately made space for mental illness, which of course we're still working on.

But two years later, after I'd had another baby and faced those obtrusive and fatalistic feelings once again, my people took notice. This wasn't a blip on the radar, and it wasn't something we could explain away—I was struggling. Our life came to a halt, and my husband abandoned his immediate plans for church planting to take a more stable job so he could support me. My mom began driving four hours round trip once a week to watch my kids while I saw a therapist. My friends stopped by to check on me when Nick was gone. I needed every bit of that support and much more to come out on the other side.

I needed to process my emotions and I needed the people in my life to make space for those complex emotions. I needed compassion for myself and from others. I needed to understand what my body was going through (hormones, adrenal fatigue, birth trauma). I needed time and space to talk and to process wounds of the past that, having never been healed, were turning into stumbling stones and strongholds. I needed to let the air hit my feelings rather than keep them inside like poison, terrified of what would happen if they were to escape.

So, a year later, when my healing felt fresh and it was time for us to move and serve at another church, I was tender, to say the least. Tender but determined to stay in freedom, I knew that constantly trying to conform to whatever church community we were in had been part of my undoing. I had exhausted myself by continually shape-shifting into whatever version of a Christian woman was expected of me in every new community: a crunchy stay-at-home mom here, a spunky career girl in the next. I couldn't do it anymore. I wouldn't do it anymore. This had to be a season of health and freedom.

Imagine how completely confused and disheartened I was when we'd been at our church for just a few short weeks and I found out the unofficial men's group had a fun little song they sang about emotions.

"What do we do with our feelings?" one man would chant.

"Shove! Them! Down!" the others would reply.

When I heard about this, I was shocked and concerned about the fellowship we had just joined. As much as I didn't want to ruffle feathers in this new space, I knew immediately I was going to be going against the grain here. I'd just gotten my head above water after years of unprocessed emotions had left me in a place of utter burnout. Because, unfortunately, what most professionals (medical and psychological) will tell us is this: Ignoring our emotions does not give us energy; it actually makes us feel much heavier.

We'll repeat what we don't repair.

We'll carry what we don't confront.

Any attempt to shove down our feelings will ultimately backfire; we'll feel them more intensely when we ignore them up front.

You Don't Shoot the Messenger

A few years later, when we'd moved from that community and planted our own church, I was regularly posting spiritual musings on social media. Then one night, feeling a little self-righteous and intelligent, I posted a graphic that said, "Feelings are liars," with a caption that pontificated on the importance of Scripture and truth over emotions and fleeting sentiments. I'll never forget the post because of the honest correction I received from one wise woman shortly after. In short, she messaged me to say she understood what I was trying to say but that I was making a blanket statement that was more harmful than helpful.

This overgeneralization I was making, that our feelings are liars, was potentially just as harmful as the "shove them down" song. The real kicker wasn't just that it rubbed people the wrong way or that calling our feelings unworthy of attention isn't the most compassionate way to approach people. The serious problem with a post like that is this: It's not entirely true. It might have been pithy, but it was only a half-truth, and half-truths never make for good theology.

I had been making a point based on observing my toddlers at the time: Their feelings that they were being unjustly treated by being asked to take naps were not the most indicative of their reality.

But we're not toddlers, and while our feelings aren't finite fixtures of truth, I've come a long way from distrusting mine. Now, instead of seeing my emotions as fact or fiction, I like to see them as messengers. These electrochemical signals, a mixture of peptides and the power of God, spread throughout my brain and body and send me alerts about how I perceive what is happening around me. Emotions are messengers, and what is the cliché we know and love?

You don't shoot the messenger.

You don't blame the emotions for being there.

Our options as they pertain to our feelings are to process them, ignore them, or obey them. Let's explore what each of these options could look like and what impact they'll have on our lives.

Dealing with the Emotion Elephant

Why does any of this matter? And what does any of this have to do with the fact that you're so tired you can't take it anymore?

The elephant in the room is taking up all the air.

The elephant in the room—our emotions that need processing—is exhausting us, mind, body, and spirit.

The elephant in the room—our subsequent capacity to use our God-given insight to decipher whatever messages our emotions bring—leaves us exhausted and at a new level of fatigue. We even have a name for it: "I can't even."

In the Bible, we see unprocessed emotions wreak havoc on the people of God.

Eve doesn't process her potential doubt that God will provide for her, and she sins.

Adam doesn't adequately process his disappointment and conviction over Eve eating the fruit, which comes out as blame.

Cain could have used a quick feelings check-in before he murdered Abel, fueled by his jealousy.

It's hard not to imagine Noah getting drunk because the ark and the flood were *traumatic*. Maybe someone could have just let him talk it out? I don't know, man.

Abram called his wife, Sarai, his sister in a foreign land because he was scared and doubtful.

David was constantly in his feelings—from lust to fear to murderous longings.

But we also see evidence—from humans and God—of emotions harnessed and processed and of His glory. We see healthy displays of emotion from God the Father, a reminder that we're made in His image:

Our Father honors and loves His kids (Isa. 43:4).

Our Father has compassion (Ps. 103:13).

Our Father is angry at injustice (Ezek. 5:13).

God the Father feels jealousy for His own glory (Exod. 34:14).

And from our Friend and Savior, Jesus, we see emotions and feelings on display.

Jesus shows empathy for sinners just before He dies (Luke 23:34).

We're told He could experience grief (Isa. 53:3) and great joy (Luke 10:21).

He was not unacquainted with anger (Matt. 23:33; John 2:14–17).

Emotions in and of themselves don't have an innate moral weight, but how we steward them can either bless or burden our lives.

Don't get me wrong—some feelings can absolutely be interconnected with sin or expressed with sinful actions. I'm specifically thinking about lust or pride. But we can't assume that they're all bad and worth dismissing. Let's keep unpacking.

The definition of *sin* is any offense against God's law. There are typically two types of sin: things we do (commission) and things we don't do (omission). While we know that Jesus came not to abolish the law but to fulfill it, we can look at the Old Testament guidelines, or commandments, to get another glimpse of what emotional sin can look like.

When we look at the Ten Commandments, the original blueprint given to Moses for living within God's good boundaries and borders (see Exod. 20:1–17), right off the bat we see a few potential sins linked to feelings.

The easiest example is, "You shall not covet." The full text tells us not to covet our neighbor's house, spouse, or belongings. Just FYI, this means Pinterest and/or social media are minefields of potential sin for many of us, amen? The word here for *covet* is the Hebrew word *chamad*, which means "to desire or take pleasure in." The good news is this: I think we can keep using social media if we deal with our hearts. Because if we leave every space where we could potentially covet, we won't have anywhere to go! Let's walk this out together.

My sister has a beautiful home. I mean *beautiful*. Her house was recently featured in a home-and-design magazine, with her picture on the front cover. I love my home, but the houses in my neighborhood are less likely to be in a magazine, and to be flat-out honest, I don't have the same skills she has for keeping her place looking immaculate. The girl has seven kids, and I promise you, I've never seen a pillow out of place. It's her spiritual gift.

So, when I visit her house, do I often feel jealous? Yes. Do I experience the emotion of desiring those same things for myself?

Yes. Do I even feel pangs of resentment and bitterness on a very unhealthy day, wishing I had what she had? Absolutely.

If I write off these feelings immediately as sin, then I'm more prone to shutting them down and getting them out as fast as I can. But if I greet them as messengers, I might actually learn something about what's going on in my heart and what I need to do next. Feelings can be symptoms of sin or precursors to sin, but they are not necessarily sinful in and of themselves. Negative feelings are a symptom of living in a fallen humanity, a broken world.

Before I ever go to my sister's house and feel a pang of jealousy, I have an issue that needs sorting. I might be experiencing a lack of gratitude for what God's given me or maybe even a need for awareness about being patient in all seasons. I'd venture to say, since we're talking about my sin here, that in this case I probably need to wrestle down some tension in my heart about where my treasure is—on earth or in heaven.

But now I'm here and I'm feeling jealous, and it's too late to fix the belief that led me to this feeling. It's OK because the emotion can also guide me to respond worshipfully in the next moments. Here's how my inner dialogue could go:

Dang, her house is so beautiful.
I wish my house were so beautiful.
Why her and not me?
Whoosh—where did that jealousy come from?
Hold on, let me pay attention to this.
What do I know to be true?
How do I want to respond?
God has done and will always do good for me.
God has drawn the boundary lines in pleasant places for me.
My treasure is not on earth; it's in heaven.
And what's more—I have so many earthly gifts that I don't deserve.
And . . . I love her. And I want good for her.

Father, I'm sorry for the way I've been seeing this.
Thanks for what you gave her, and thanks for what you gave me.

Then I can use my mouth to bless God and bless her and say, "Katie, your house looks phenomenal. And you take such good care of it. Teach me your ways!"

Is that a pretty lengthy inner monologue? Well, kind of. The whole thing can happen in just a few seconds. But the good news is, the more we do this work, paying attention to our emotions, the quicker it gets.

The most important thing I hope you hear is that the feeling is a messenger telling me something could be potentially off in my belief—or a feeling could indicate that something is very right in your belief, even if that feeling is negative. But negative feelings are not necessarily a sin; they're a physical response of electrochemical signals alerting our brain and body to the fact that we live in a fallen world and are out of agreement with God's perspective. Which means that if we're truly listening, feelings can become powerful prompts for getting *back* into alignment with God.

Psalm 4:4 puts it this way: "Be angry, and do not sin; ponder in your own hearts on your beds, and be silent" (ESV). The anger can be present without the sins of omission or commission. What happens after the anger—our response through action— is where sin comes in if we're not attentive.

If we use this tactic with other emotions, it could look like this:

Be sad, but don't despair.

Be joyful but not proud.

Experience fear, but choose courage anyhow.

Feel your feelings of grief, but don't believe for a second that God has left you.

It's OK to be frustrated, but don't lose hope.

We could go on and on, but healthily processing your emotions will often look like experiencing them, noticing where they've come from, and then allowing truth to help you move through the feelings.

The Body Keeps the Score

As I mentioned earlier, we have the opportunity to respond to our feelings in three main ways: process, ignore, or obey. The last two options take less intention on the front end but wreak havoc on our lives, brains, bodies, and energy levels.

We can ignore our emotions or "Shove! Them! Down!" like those guys I once knew. We hear a story like that and think it's preposterous, yet we all do this all the time. In many ways, our culture conditions us (especially women) to pretend as if emotions don't exist or that they are a liability. We feel shame for crying— I'm not sure women apologize for anything more than they do for their tears. We feel shame for our anger when often what we're angry at is actual injustice—and it makes God angry too. We feel shame for our fear, as if it's not a natural response to living in a terrifying world.

And what's more—we're often praised for living lives devoid of emotion. Our culture praises women for being composed, chill, and easygoing. We refer to women as strong if they can make it through a funeral without breaking down in tears, as if crying negates the incredible power required of us to adequately navigate grief. Businesswomen who can get through their days devoid of emotion are praised for their stoicism, as if feeling nothing is a requirement to be a compelling and successful leader. Mothers who never acknowledge their own fears, frustrations, and physical needs are glorified, as if God intended motherhood to be a space where we forget our own boundaries and borders.

The problem with our glorification of emotionless living is that it sets a standard no one can actually live up to. Whether the expectation that we'll stuff it down is spoken or not, we all begin to see this as the ideal.

If you're skeptical of this theory, think back to the last time you saw a woman cry around other people. If there were two people or two hundred in the room, I'm willing to bet that one of the first things she said as the tears slipped from her face was "Sorry I'm crying" or "I'm not sure why I'm crying" or "I'm such a mess, sorry." We apologize instinctively for our tears because we've believed the cultural lie that pushing through and ignoring them is a worthy pursuit.

Is the initial process of ignoring emotions easier than pausing to make space and process them? Sure. It takes less time. But unprocessed emotions never stay that way. Unprocessed emotions imbed themselves in our souls and bodies, costing us so much more than the short time it would have taken to give them a little air and speak a little truth over them.

Let's start with the body first. As a reminder, emotions are electrochemical signals. While we talk a good deal about our heart as if it's some unseeable entity, feelings are a scientific, perceivable physical experience. Our Father was so kind as to give our bodies an outlet to release this emotional energy. Think about how making space for tears, laughter, movement, physical comfort, dancing, wringing your hands, pacing the floors, or pounding your fists makes you feel when emotions are high. It's a release, a relief.

But when there is no release or relief, our body stores that energy as inflammation or tension. Studies have shown that unprocessed stress, grief, sadness, and anger can lead to everything from TMJ to heart disease. The bestselling book *The Body Keeps the Score* by Dr. Bessel van der Kolk is an incredible, long-form explanation that unpacks the effect of trauma on our physical bodies. But what I appreciate most about the book is how the title validates what many of us have been feeling for a very long time: Unprocessed emotion will take a toll on our flesh. Our feelings and the way we ignore them leave us exhausted.

We were taught and shown how to hide our emotions and praised for doing so. But it is not working, and it is leaving us more tired. So, let's grow past this unhealthy coping mechanism and honor God in our good bodies. Amen?

You Can't Help How You Feel (Maybe You Can)

I was speaking on a panel about relationships at a church over fifteen years ago when another woman on the panel said something that made me bristle. It wasn't all that crazy, but it impacted me enough that I still think about it today—so that's something. She was telling a story about her life and said that we can't help who we fall in love with. The hairs on the back of my neck stood up, but I didn't say anything. I just kept going with the rest of the panel.

This was in the early 2000s, and all the Christian girls I knew were very concerned about falling for someone who didn't love God as much as they did or someone with whom they were not "equally yoked." This phrase comes from 2 Corinthians 6:14, which says, "Do not be yoked together with unbelievers. For what do righteousness and wickedness have in common? Or what fellowship can light have with darkness?"

And here was this wise woman I loved and respected telling women they couldn't help who they fell in love with. Where was the balance? Where was the truth?

For almost two decades, I've walked with many women through dating and marriage, and I've learned a lot about being unequally yoked—just not in the ways I thought I would. I felt unequally yoked when I hired someone for my business who didn't carry our culture or heart for women. I felt unequally yoked when I made an every-single-day-of-the-week workout rhythm with someone who was not a life speaker or an encourager. But in all my watching, I've decided we can help ourselves when it comes to falling in love with people who don't share our same passion for faith.

If you find yourself attracted to someone who doesn't love God, the first thing to notice is that, like with jealousy, there is probably an unhelpful belief underneath the attraction. In this case, I'd say it's the understanding of what makes a good spouse or a healthy union. If that belief is unexamined and established first, it will guide your emotions. However, there is still—there is always—a choice to be made.

In the end, I think that's what bothered me most about this woman's claim that we can't help who we fall in love with. Because she might as well have said that we can't help but carry through our emotions into our actions, that our feelings somehow speak our destiny, and this is neither true nor good news.

We get to ask: Is this relationship wise for me? Do I want to act on my attraction? Will acting on this attraction leave me in agreement with my nearness to God, or will it make me feel further away?

If we couldn't help who we fell in love with, no marriage would have any hope. We'd all just be swapping partners like life is one long episode of *Grey's Anatomy*, you know what I mean?

We often can't help our emotions. But we can help whether or not we choose to obey them.

I wake up and feel discouraged about a conversation I had with a friend yesterday. I can obey that emotion, keep fuming the whole morning, and pick a fight with her the next time I see her.

I feel mad at the guy who cut me off in traffic, and I have the option to obey that emotion, lay on my horn, let out a cuss word, and then pull up next to him and realize he goes to our church.

I feel abandoned by God and hopeless when I sit with my mom in the doctor's office for a diagnosis. I can obey that feeling and speak death over both of us, continuing the thought pattern that He is vengeful and hateful toward us.

I feel left out when I open Instagram and see a few gals from my Bible study get together without me. I have the option to obey that feeling of bitterness and move into the rest of the day, rejecting others before they reject me.

None of these feelings are broken in and of themselves: wanting communion with others, feeling frustrated at small injustices, wanting wholeness and healing for those we love, and desiring to be loved and included. But we do have the option to process these emotions and then choose either a worshipful response or an unhealthy one.

This matters immensely, for those of us who are tired of being tired, if our default mode is to obey the unhealthy impulse our emotions lead us toward.

I have a small tattoo on my left ring finger that others can only see if I'm gesticulating wildly with my hands. But I can see it all the time from my vantage point. It's on the inner part, where my ring finger and middle finger meet, and it's just one small, thin line. I got it to remind me of Matthew 7:13–14: "Enter through the narrow gate. For wide is the gate and broad is the road that leads to destruction, and many enter through it. But small is the gate and narrow the road that leads to life, and only a few find it."

These words of Jesus remind me that His way, the way to life, health, and wholeness, often takes more delicate and intentional decision-making than the path that leads to destruction. And so it goes with our emotions. The path of reacting and responding to and obeying our feelings is broad—we'll find so many unhealthy options and friends along the way. But the destruction that is stirred up in our soul and our life will leave us exhausted every single time.

We can't help how we feel. We do not choose the emotions that rise in our brains and bodies. But we do have a choice about how we speak into the beliefs that produced those emotions, and we do have a choice about how we respond to them after they're felt. We have a choice. Let's choose the narrow way that leads to life.

What If You Could?

If we want to fight emotional exhaustion, the narrow path that will lead us to more energy and abundant life is experiencing our emotions. We cannot shove them down or pretend they don't exist, and we cannot obey them mindlessly as if they're always rooted in goodness and truth.

In the next chapter, we'll talk about how we can practically, healthily process our feelings, but I want to paint a picture of hope for you if you find yourself in the throes of emotional fatigue. This kind of tiredness presents itself in a lack of motivation, physical soreness, feelings of hopelessness, apathy, headaches, trouble sleeping, irrational anger or grief, and a myriad of other issues. If these symptoms or others have become severe and unavoidable, I cannot encourage you strongly enough to see the resource page in the back of this book to get help. Letting someone else come alongside you is not weak but incredibly wise and God-honoring.

And I want to leave you with a story of what happened to me right before I got help for the first time.

When I was in the throes of postpartum depression, I didn't know it. To compound this, I had unprocessed emotions—probably from my whole life but particularly from the season of motherhood that had hit me like a freight train—and I had very few tools or the awareness to process them. My newest baby was just over a year old, but I also had a three-year-old and a two-year-old. I was physically tired, but there were so many emotional issues at play—I just didn't know where to start.

I had gone on a bachelorette weekend trip for one of my best friends, Stephanie, and to be honest, I'd intentionally tried very hard to impress everyone with how well I was doing. I wanted them to see me as a strong, resilient young mom who had it all together and had oodles of sage advice and wisdom to share. I brought my Bible and journal so everyone would see me having my quiet time in the living room when they got up. I went on an eight-mile run so they'd be impressed that I hadn't "let go of myself" (deep groan), and I abstained from having any wine at dinner. The truth was, I didn't have enough money for a glass of wine, but I wanted them to think it was because I was super holy.

On the drive back, when I thought I'd done a killer job of seeming like I had it all together, my two best friends, Laura and Stephanie, told me something jarring. They said that one of the other gals on the trip had come to them asking if I was OK. She said I seemed depressed. I was shocked and a little mad and used my favorite party line, "I'm just tired! I have three small kids! I'm great—just tired." I was sitting in the back seat (showing how servant-hearted I was), and Steph and Laura were up front. They exchanged a look when I gave my defensive rebuttal.

"Do you guys think I'm not OK? Do you think I'm depressed?" I asked in disbelief.

What followed was one of the holiest, most sacred, and tenderest interventions I could describe or imagine. They took turns lovingly sharing examples of how I didn't seem physically tired but broken and exhausted in other ways. Still, I kept rebuffing their observations. Eventually, Laura took another tactic and started telling me about her recent bout of depression and how God had used physical and supernatural means to help her feel better.

The way she described the relief she was feeling broke open a well of awareness, grief, and wild hope in me. And from the back seat, my voice broke halfway through this sentence: "You mean . . . I could . . . feel better?"

By the time I got the words out, I had begun sobbing, and I wouldn't stop for another hour. We spent the rest of the drive strategizing in regard to how I'd talk to my husband about how I was doing and what steps I would take next to get help and healing.

That car ride changed my life.

Through therapy, prayer, medicine, exercise, and time, I experienced a renewal that had an indescribably deep and wide effect. I had so many emotions that I'd needed to experience and process, and my friends gave me the permission and freedom to listen to what my overwhelming feelings had to say rather than stuff them down. What I learned in that season still equips me to stay emotionally healthy. God used that fight against depression to help me healthily process the feelings of shame and inadequacy that will continue to crop up for the rest of my human life. I also began to understand the damage I'd be doing to my body, mind, and spirit if I insisted on ignoring my emotions. I believe this is a truth I'll be learning, in the most life-giving way, for the rest of my life.

We all say that we "can't even."

We all are susceptible to the lie that we'll be or seem stronger if we push through and ignore our emotions.

We feel like we don't have time to feel or give space to our anger, grief, joy, and confusion.

But our emotions are dealing with us if we don't deal with them. Our emotions are driving us, exhausting us, when we leave them unprocessed.

We feel like we can't even—but what if we could?

What if we could slow down, listen to our emotions, let our bodies process them, let our minds trace where they came from, and determine where we want them to go? What if we could even?

Wouldn't that change our lives?

Reflection Questions

1. What is your typical response to emotions: process, ignore, or obey?
2. How do unprocessed emotions show up in your life?
3. Do you have any fear in regard to experiencing your emotions?
4. What messages have you received overtly or subtly about how to handle your feelings?

Symptoms of Emotional Exhaustion in Our Lives

- Irritability
- Apathy
- Unprovoked tears or anger
- Physical fatigue or soreness
- Depression
- Sense of dread or hopelessness

Verses to Meditate On

Psalm 73:26

My flesh and my heart may fail,
but God is the strength of my heart
and my portion forever.

2 Corinthians 12:9

And He has said to me, "My grace is sufficient for you, for power is perfected in weakness." Most gladly, therefore, I will rather boast about my weaknesses, so that the power of Christ may dwell in me. (NASB1995)

Psalm 34:17-19

The righteous cry, and the LORD hears
and delivers them out of all their troubles.
The LORD is near to the brokenhearted
and saves those who are crushed in spirit.

Many are the afflictions of the righteous,
but the LORD delivers him out of them all. (NASB1995)

twelve

emotional exhaustion

"I am loved and cared for."

We were on one of those friendship walks that had started with the simple aim of catching up and moving our bodies but had gone much deeper. As we walked, mile after mile, our conversation went deeper into the parts of our lives where we were both struggling. My friend Kristen has changed my life for the better these past few years, and a handful of our walks have been world-shifting.

What I love most about Kristen is that we're almost unlikely friends; you might not pair us up as soul sisters if you knew us separately, but God has undoubtedly tied our hearts together. Kristen is the curious to my adamant, the tempered to my tough, and the peace to my passion. But neither of us wants the other to become who we are, primarily because our opposites-attract thing means we get to learn from one another.

Kristen is also a therapist, and when I introduce her, I usually joke about how I wish she were my therapist. But you can imagine after how I've described her that she's a healthy boundary setter. So with that, I've never felt like she's actually trying to be my therapist. She's just an incredibly wise and thoughtful friend.

"Have you ever thought about creating a container for your sadness?"

She asked this question as we rounded the corner, hitting the three-miles-walked marker. I wasn't quite sure what she meant, so I asked for clarification. What followed changed my life.

"Stop me if I'm wrong, but Jess—I think you'd say this about yourself too. You're the kind of gal who can seem like you're expressing emotion, but that's just on the top layer. There's a lot beneath the surface that doesn't get out."

I nodded. I've known this was true for the last decade or so. People assume I'm being incredibly vulnerable when, in reality, I'm being incredibly guarded.

She continued. "Again, take this or leave it. But I wonder if all that emotion beneath the surface needs to get out. I wonder if much of it is sadness and if that's very scary for you to access."

She was right again. I reminded her that since I had gotten healing from depression over a dozen years earlier, I'd felt almost allergic to sadness. I didn't want to sit with it again after staring it in the face for too long. I didn't necessarily feel shame about my deepest emotions, but I explained to Kristen that I worried that if they hit the air and saw the light of day, I'd never be able to do anything but *feel*.

If I welcomed my sadness and grief to the table, the overwhelming loss I felt about everything (from my recent health trials to people leaving our church to the baby we'd lost ten years earlier) would swallow me whole. If I cracked the lid on my fear (ranging from pandemic leftovers to whether or not my kids would follow Jesus and/or questioning whether we were wasting our lives in ministry) and made space for it, I wouldn't have space for anything else. I was even dubious about my joy and passion; it felt like too much to access and live normally.

"That's why I'm suggesting a container for your emotions— a space, maybe even a physical place or a strategic time, where you can feel with God. Of course, eventually, the goal would be accessing your honest feelings more frequently, but this would be a great start. And the most important thing is that if you don't make a container for your feelings, they will leak out everywhere and impact everything, maybe in ways you don't like."

She was right.

I wasn't keeping my emotions locked away where they could never affect anyone, me included. Instead, my unintentional decision not to give space to my feelings was causing them to come out at inopportune times and in subconscious ways. And more than that, lugging around this figurative vault of emotions was exhausting me in every way.

I had containers that had worked well for me, but I wasn't being intentional to take full advantage of them. I'd taken up running fifteen years prior, in the thick of postpartum depression, as a way to be alone, feel, think, and talk to God. I'd utilized therapy in challenging seasons as a space to process my emotions, but what about on regular days? What about normal seasons?

I realized I needed everyday containers for my everyday grief, frustration, and even joy. As a pastor, a leader, a boss, and a mother, it was easy for me to be on everyone else's team and harder for me to carve out spaces for my own emotions. I used Kristen's insight to establish smaller and more practical containers for my emotions: daily gratitude journaling, weekly worship sessions where I could make space for my grief or anger with God, and even more intentional check-ins with my friends and family.

What I found was that when I stopped normalizing stuffing my emotions, I didn't need such significant containers—smaller ones worked wonders.

Curious Compassion

Many of us are emotionally exhausted. We are so worn down and drained from life that we cannot process or contain our basic everyday feelings. This may present itself in our being overly emotional, lacking control over how we express our emotions, or—on the other end of the spectrum—being so emotionally exhausted that we cannot access our feelings easily.

Maybe you find yourself tearing up as soon as you walk into church, and you're unsure why. Maybe you scream at your kids even though they didn't do anything wrong, and you can't figure out why you lost it. You might be the kind of gal everyone thinks is a pure ray of sunshine, but you turn into a raging bull behind the car's wheel. It could be that only your roommate, your husband, or your therapist hears the emotional barrage that's been welling up inside of you.

Or maybe you wonder when you last cried because it sure wasn't in the recent past. You could struggle to express affection to the people you deeply love because it makes you feel unsafe or insecure. Maybe it's easy for you to scoff or judge other people who seem to have very emotional expressions in their worship of God, but secretly you wonder if there's something wrong with you. I wonder if some people in your life have asked for more words, more access, more vulnerability, and if that feels like the one thing you don't have to offer.

Maybe you're somewhere in the middle of those two, or you swing wildly between both sides. The great news is this: With God's help, we can learn a new way to experience our emotions, rooted in His love and care for us. The presence of God, the throne room of grace, is the safest container for our emotions. And we have access to it at all times, by grace through faith.

As we're looking for a healthy way to approach our emotions, we don't need to look further than our kind and caring Father, who makes space for us and our feelings. Even if emotions overwhelm us, there is no feeling we experience that is too much for God. So, if you've assumed that walking with God is about emotionless and stoic faith, now is the time to rewrite that story. Or if you've been taught, subtly or overtly, that God finds your feelings insignificant or distracting—I'm excited for the renewal we're all about to experience.

When I consider your heavens,
　　the work of your fingers,
the moon and the stars,
　　which you have set in place,
what is mankind that you are mindful of them,
　　human beings that you care for them? (Ps. 8:3–4)

Are not two sparrows sold for a penny? Yet not one of them will fall to the ground outside your Father's care. And even the very hairs of your head are all numbered. So don't be afraid; you are worth more than many sparrows. (Matt. 10:29–31)

He who did not spare his own Son, but gave him up for us all—how will he not also, along with him, graciously give us all things? (Rom. 8:32)

Cast all your anxiety on him because he cares for you. (1 Pet. 5:7)

God is not dismissive of our feelings. Instead, He compassionately moves toward us to be there for us as we experience this world. I love learning about Greek and Hebrew words, and the word *mercy* is no exception.

Come with me if you've never heard a description of the difference between mercy and grace. If you've heard this a million times, let's ask God for fresh eyes.

Let's first look at Ephesians 2:4–5, which mentions both:

But because of his great love for us, God, who is rich in mercy, made us alive with Christ even when we were dead in transgressions—it is by grace you have been saved.

God's mercy is His compassionate approach toward His kids, which we love. I've heard Bible scholars share about how in both Hebrew and Greek, it's an active word that denotes movement and coming down toward. God's mercy is when we're absolved from the punishment we deserve. Simply put, mercy is when we don't get what we deserve (death for our sin), and grace is when we get what we don't deserve (compassion from the Father we often sin against).

Grace is when we get a fresh start after losing it in an argument and forgetting to direct our emotions in the way they should go. Mercy is when God the Father offers comfort to us, even amid those emotions (and potential sin), because He loves us and wants to be there for us no matter what.

If God is continually compassionate and merciful toward your emotions, never dismissive or frustrated that you're still a feeling human, might it be time to choose the same compassion for yourself? And can we take it one step further?

I propose we choose compassionate curiosity as an approach to our feelings. Compassionate curiosity is not beating ourselves up, shaming ourselves, or trying to stuff our feelings down but rather paying attention to them with interested hearts to figure out why they've arrived. Compassionate curiosity isn't obeying every feeling. It's not blindly following every feeling to destruction—but instead noticing it, naming it, and discerning the best way to move forward.

Let's walk through this:

Notice what you feel as the emotion hits. How does the anger, excitement, fear, disappointment, or other feeling appear in your body? Notice it with God, involve Him in the process, and ask Holy Spirit to help you discern where this emotion might be coming from and what's making it so strong, or track when you often find yourself experiencing this feeling.

Name the emotion as best you can. Don't fear using nonfeeling words, metaphors, or other adjectives to get as specific as possible. If it's as straightforward as "jealousy," you can just use that word. But if it's as subtle as "a sticky sadness twinged with fear," that's great too. I remember once describing my grief as "pinching rather than punching," and the friend I was speaking to immediately understood what I was trying to convey. Give yourself the same space to name what it is you're experiencing.

Finally, take time to discern the wisest way to move forward concerning this emotion. Does it need confession because it came from an unhealthy or unholy root belief? Do you need to sit with God and allow Him to comfort you? Is there something you can or should do to take a step to resolve a conflict or issue that's causing the emotion? Do you need to let it go or talk it out with someone else? What is God saying to you about this feeling?

Compassionate curiosity is the way to look at your emotions without judging them while also giving yourself space to determine how to move forward in the most worshipful way. In the next chapter, we'll talk about some rhythms for your life that might give you space to better use this tactic to fight emotional exhaustion.

Let It Out

I recently read a book that gave language and insight to issues I've been struggling with my entire life—and statistically, so have you.

When I came across the book *Burnout* by Emily Nagoski and Amelia Nagoski, I was so incredibly grateful. Specifically, the scientific evidence I read about completing the stress cycle changed my life.

The book's premise is that women process stress differently than men, that many of us suffer from what the Nagoskis call "human giver syndrome," and that we need a scientific solution to process the emotional and mental stress that our bodies are holding on to.[1] Human giver syndrome is the false belief that women have an obligation to be pretty, happy, calm, generous, and attentive to the needs of others. If we don't process this often-unspoken obligation, we'll suffer from burnout—a level of emotional, physical, and mental fatigue that takes extensive work to repair. We'll live lives of reactive defeat, assuming that exhaustion is the norm and never fully feeling capable and ready for our days.

The Nagoskis' scientific premise is that our bodies need to complete the stress cycle. As a result, they need an outlet to process emotions. They suggest a host of ideas: breathing, running, laughing, crying, or utilizing a creative outlet. For example, after doing some of my own digging, I found out that crying literally releases oxytocin in our brains. It's a God-given, built-in, scientifically proven way to relieve pain and stress.

Here's an example of what this has looked like in my life: After reading *Burnout* a year ago, I started taking my running journey more seriously. I've been running since I began to fight postpartum depression almost fifteen years ago, and the practice is one of the containers I use to feel. I often cry on runs, I always sort out my thoughts, and I don't know that I've ever returned from a run feeling more emotionally conflicted than when I left.

But what happens when I can't go on a run? Good question.

A few nights ago, my husband and I got into an argument. It was our first in a long while, and as arguments go, it wasn't explosive. We've been married seventeen years, together as a couple for over twenty years, and we've learned how to fight pretty healthily.

In this particular argument, I was angry at him. I felt like he hadn't backed me up during a disagreement with one of our kids. He saw my perspective, and I saw his. He apologized and asked what he could do to correct it . . . but it didn't matter. My body was on fire with anger. I felt like there were probably lightning bolts coming out of my fingertips, and even though he was so calm, levelheaded, and humble—I really wanted to scream at him.

We sat on the sectional sofa in our living room with a chasm between us. He knew I was still agitated, and he was calmly waiting and watching to see what to do next.

The truth was, I was feeling shame and condemnation, not just about the conversation that had just taken place but about three other instances that had happened that day with our kids. In multiple encounters, the kids had overtly or subtly deeply disrespected me. That's not an uncommon experience, but neither is it uncommon for teens to be disrespectful as they figure out their footing in life. However, I had taken each of those moments personally, and by the time Nick and I talked, I was feeling all over the place.

As he sat and watched me quietly, I tried to take deep breaths and sort out those emotions and why they were so strong. I even thought, *I wish I could go for a run*, as I inhaled and exhaled and let myself feel around in the darkest part of my soul to see where the injury was.

And then, it just exploded. I hadn't told Nick about the other three occurrences that day, and as I internally processed and found the condemnation and shame inside me, I started crying. And I kept crying. And I started talking, telling him about the day, as I cried. And he listened and showed me compassion, telling me how sorry he was that had happened. And when all the tears were out, I sat with my eyes closed, inhaled deeply, and noticed how much better I felt.

I couldn't go on a run at 10:00 p.m., but my body needed another release: tears.

Sometimes it might be yelling (I suggest yelling alone at first so you don't say something you regret—I've learned this the hard way), sometimes it might be crying, or sometimes you might need to run or dance or stomp like a two-year-old (I also suggest being alone for this one).

Whatever your particular release of choice is for today's specific emotion—your body needs a release. Likewise, your feelings need to take up space in your physical life in a way that will help you complete the emotional stress cycle.

Phone a Friend

Sometimes we just need to talk it out. We can take full advantage of the presence and power of God that is alive and active in the humans around us. I love to talk it out with my people, so I hate to give caveats about this form of processing our emotions. But while I love being a good-news girl who talks more about the solution than the problem, we need to address a few of the processing pitfalls that feed our emotional exhaustion instead of aiding in our peace.

Verbally processing our emotions becomes unhealthy or potentially harmful when we share with people who are not safe or who should not be trusted. This can be a painful game of trial and error, or we can be wise and slow to speak before we see the fruit of wisdom and trust in someone else's life. So, here are a few questions to ask before you share the depths of your emotion with someone else:

- Does this person gossip, share secrets, or generally tend to be loose-lipped? Remember that if they share secrets with you, that may mean they're not best suited to keep your feelings and experiences private.
- Does this person live wisely and receive wisdom from others?
- Does this person apply grace and truth well in the circumstances? Will they use condemnation or shame as a tool against you, or will they shy away from speaking counsel when you need it?
- Have you already processed with multiple people? It can be helpful to get different perspectives on what you're going through, but often too many voices will leave us feeling more confused and unclear. And worse, they can leave us feeling vulnerable and exposed in an unhelpful way.
- Is any part of you choosing to process this information with this person in particular in an attempt to manipulate the situation, get them on your side, or bond from the angst or frustration?
- Most notably, is the information you're about to share so tender that it might be better suited for a mental health professional, trusted pastor, or doctor? Essentially, by asking the person to process with you, are you asking them to go above their capacity in holding your pain with you?

I am not trying to be the processing police. I am trying to make the experience of processing your emotions so fruitful that you keep going back for more.

I have had so many moments when sharing what was happening within me emotionally felt like the best possible next step until I realized I had lit my fire without a fireplace. The pain I experienced in the aftermath would have been avoidable if I'd chosen a different person to process with. Talk about exhausting. Nothing is more tiring than a challenging emotional moment multiplied and complicated when all you wanted to do was feel better.

I am a person who needs to process, even when I think I don't need to. I'll have an issue seemingly worked out in my head, only to find that I get much more clarity when I chat with a wise friend.

In the back of this book, you'll find resources to find a therapist, and if no one else in your life has ever vouched for the power of finding a safe counselor or mental health professional, it's my honor to do so. I've been seeing a counselor, in some form, on and off for the last fifteen years. And the part that never gets old is having one hour just to *talk*. Most professionals I've worked with have been light on advice and heavy on listening. The magic, for me, has been in having a shame-free space to say everything I'm feeling. And often my healing is bound up in the processing, how I trace and track my emotions and make sense of what God is doing in my heart and mind.

Whether it's with a friend, a professional, a pastor, a spouse, a sibling, or your journal, let's embrace the power of processing, so our emotions don't continue to weigh us down needlessly.

Environmental Factors

Another important consideration when processing our emotions is our actual physical environment. You and I are spiritual beings who live in a physical world, where certain behaviors, lifestyle factors, and stimuli have a genuine impact on our emotions.

As we acknowledge some of these factors, I'm calling a "No Judgment Zone." There's no shame in noticing how environmental factors could be influencing your behavior. No condemnation here, but let's be honest with ourselves so we can see some relief and change in our lives. See if you've ever used any of the following phrases:

"Sorry for what I said when I was hungry."

"I thought I was depressed and then realized I just needed some vitamin D."

"I know I was a little punchy last night. Red wine does that to me."

"It seemed like my life was a mess, and then I realized I just had PMS."

"I couldn't stop crying or figure out what was wrong, and then I remembered I only slept three hours last night."

Here's the deal: No amount of emotional or spiritual maturity can make us immune to the environmental factors impacting how we feel. I don't care how much you talk to Jesus, if you're rolling on three hours of sleep, your cortisol is out of whack, and if you have a headache from forgetting to bring your sunglasses, you will feel a little crazy.

Emotionally awake people don't try to pretend environmental factors don't exist, but instead they pay attention to the factors that impact them and adjust accordingly.

Nobody likes to be asked if they're on their period when they're experiencing heightened emotions, and nobody really should be asking, for that matter. But you and I can open our eyes to what is happening in our hormones so we can be prepared when problems feel larger than life. We can take vitamins and supplements to support our hormones, eat foods that aid in our body's process of menstruation, and in general be a little gentler on ourselves during this time of the month.

We get to exercise autonomy when we notice that certain habits or rhythms impact our emotions in a significant way. For example, if caffeine makes you feel anxious, the blood sugar crash from processed sugar makes you feel depressed, or staying up late watching Netflix results in decreased motivation in the morning—GREAT NEWS!—this is emotional fatigue we can fix.

We get to go with God, listen to Holy Spirit and our bodies, and make the decisions that help us love and live in emotional health.

Your feelings are not only welcome here in this life, they're essential. Knowing what you feel and being able to make space for your God-given emotions is not a departure from being a spiritually mature woman of God. On the contrary, feeling your feelings with your body and your voice and directing them with compassion and truth is one of the most powerful ways you can use the authority you've been given by our Father to bring light into this world.

Our feelings are good and worthy of attention.

They deserve to be processed fully so we can keep feeling them for the rest of our beautiful, marvelous, miraculous, and messy human lives.

Let's keep going and getting more of our precious energy back from the enemy.

Tips for Emotional Low Power Mode

- Create a journaling habit. This is a great way to notice, process, and make space for your emotions.
- Pay attention to patterns in emotions. See if you can use less energy being surprised by them and instead anticipate their arrival in health.

- Ask God if He has anything He wants to share with you about _____ emotion. Listen for His voice, search His Word, and look for Him to give you insight.
- Dance it out. Just like Cristina and Meredith on *Grey's Anatomy* (if you know, you know). Put on some life-giving music and see if those emotions don't start to come to the surface.
- If you're feeling grief but have stuffed down your emotions so long you can't access them, try watching a sad movie to connect your physical and mental.
- Likewise, I suggest watching something hilarious if you have difficulty tapping into your emotions. Laughing, like crying, also stimulates endorphins.
- Play this game with some trusted friends: Send three emojis via text to tell each other how you're doing. No need for explanation, just an unapologetic emotional check-in.
- Utilize a period-tracker app or keep a quick note on your phone to anticipate and accommodate hormonal shifts.
- Consider shifting the main lifestyle factors that impact emotional health: exercise, nutrition, and alcohol consumption. While making initial changes may take effort, the energy that will be saved in the long haul will surely make this a low-power move.

What Women Have to Say

We are undergoing a year of big changes. I have been worrying about the future, worrying about my kids' adjustment, and mourning the transitions. It's helped to unload on safe people who speak truth and to also write what I feel and then write what I would say to someone else who was dealing with the same thing. Because, inevitably, I am gentler with others than I am with myself. Then I try to keep visiting those responses I have written down.

Jessie, 38, stay-at-home mom of four

thirteen

reset your rhythms

It took me four kids to figure out how to recover. I don't mean bounce back. I don't cosign on the idea of new moms "bouncing back." After bringing a life into the world, the goal shouldn't be to get your body, energy, and schedule back to exactly how they were before. Instead, we honor our lives by acknowledging where we need to make space—even in our bodies. So I didn't want to bounce back.

But I did want to recover, maybe even uncover, the parts of myself that felt sacred and whole before pregnancy. And I noticed that after having each of my first three babies, I'd really struggled to feel like myself for a very long time. No matter how hard I tried or how determined I was, I would feel so disoriented and dissociated for an extended period. I couldn't perform or maintain any of the rhythms that made me feel like the healthiest version of myself.

And then my incredibly wise and intuitive husband devised a plan after the birth of our fourth baby. He watched me struggle, just a few days after his birth, trying to do *all the things*: read my Bible, make my breakfast, lead and love my other kids, shower and get dressed, plus anything else that had helped me live an abundant life before.

So, he sat me down in love and suggested a new way. His idea was to list all the rhythms that kept me healthy and try adding one new rhythm at a time. Then, once I could conquer accomplishing that rhythm and having a newborn, I could add another. But no more of this all-at-once stuff. The list started very simple, got more complex as it progressed, and looked something like this:

1. Brush my teeth
2. Wash my face
3. Make my coffee
4. Read my Bible
5. Make my food
6. Help get the other kids dressed/bathed
7. Tidy up around the house
8. Go back to church
9. Prepare food for others
10. Grocery shop
11. Exercise
12. Spend time in community

On the first day of trying his plan, he reminded me, "Your only goal today is to brush your teeth and care for the baby. Be patient with yourself on all the other points and allow others to help you. Then, when you feel like you've got brushing your teeth and caring for the baby, we'll add washing your face."

I was flooded with two feelings: (1) I'm grateful for him, and (2) . . . this is silly; I should be able to do more.

But wouldn't you know that when I went with the plan, patiently adding in rhythms and routines rather than doing it all at once and feeling like a failure, I returned to feeling like myself more quickly. I had so much compassion for myself and felt victory celebrating all the small wins.

This is still my top tip for new moms: List all the rhythms that make you feel like yourself. Then, do not attempt to do them all the first day you're home from the hospital. Instead, take them one at a time and add another when the previous routine has become just that—routine.

I hope I didn't lose you on the childbirth part because this isn't a story about childbirth. This story is about patiently pursuing rhythms—one at a time—in Jesus's name.

A Routine That Makes Sense

I'm not sure when I first heard the distinction between schedules and rhythms, but I do know that it changed my life. The premise is straightforward: When we schedule our days, we create a rigid plan based on time. But conversely, establishing rhythms in our life creates more fluid patterns while still providing structure.

A schedule says, "I go to bed at 10:30 each night." A rhythm says, "I always wash my face and take a few minutes to journal before I go to bed." A schedule says, "I call my mom every Thursday at 10:00 a.m." A rhythm says, "I check in with my mom as I walk around the grocery store weekly. It's our best time to catch up."

Rhythms give us space to breathe, while schedules often set us up for failure. Rhythms are just routines that make sense and align with our core beliefs about what we want our lives to look like.

Here's what all of this has to do with the fact that you and I are tired of being tired: We cannot fight our spiritual, physical, mental, or emotional exhaustion without embracing rhythms of rest. And we will burn out if we try to embrace every rhythm simultaneously.

I think a huge reason why rest "doesn't work" for many of us is because we try too much too soon. And just like learning to exercise, this is a muscle we'll have to develop over time with patience.

Here's the great news: When we add rhythms of rest at a sustainable pace, we'll experience the fruit of the routine and the joy of doing something wise for ourselves. This double-sided win helps us keep the rhythm going and add in more as it's time to.

In this chapter, I want to metaphorically sit down with you, as my husband did for me, and list what matters most. Then I will take you through the progression of exhaustion-fighting tactics that seems the wisest to me. Still, ultimately, you have to exercise the authority and autonomy to make the right decisions for you.

Inventory Day

I worked retail in my twenties, and when you've worked retail, you know—nothing is worse than inventory day. But, of course, we shouldn't have called it "inventory day" because we technically did the procedure at night. Once or twice a year, as soon as the store would close, every manager and person in leadership would gear up for a night of *counting*. We'd count everything on the floor and everything in the back, checking to figure out exactly where we stood. Inventory was intense work, but it was the only way to know what we had, what we had too much of, and what we had too little of.

Before determining what rhythms we need to establish or strengthen to stop living exhausted, we need to take inventory. You've read about the different kinds of exhaustion, but how are they sitting with you? How have your feelings or beliefs shifted since you first started reading this book? Initially, you had an idea about where you were the weariest, but does it still resonate?

I've got a series of reflection questions below, and my encouragement as you take a moment to answer is this: There are no right or wrong answers, just honest ones. So, as you notice tensions or discouragements regarding your current level of exhaustion, don't feel as if you have to find the answers. When we take inventory, we're not inflating the numbers—we must know the truth about current things.

You ready? Let's go.

1. Where are you currently experiencing the most fatigue?
2. Do you think there's hope?
3. What do you feel most needs to change to get rest in this area of your life?
4. What would you do first to make that change?
5. What scares you most about taking that step?
6. Is the risk worth it to fight this exhaustion?

I'm proud of you for so bravely answering these questions. God is mighty in you. After taking some time to reflect, I pray that you feel even more ready to determine the right sequence of rhythms that will work for you to fight fatigue. Remember, we're taking it slow and steady. One slight shift at a time. Amen?

Spiritual Rhythms

Before we move on to the other forms of fatigue, let's deal with our souls. It's imperative that we don't see the list below as a checklist to accomplish *right now*. Rather, these are rhythms that we can work in, one at a time, as needed. These are not rhythms that God wants from us; they're offerings *for* us—for our good, our renewal, and our rest. Let's dive in.

- *Practice silence and solitude with God.* If you feel like you're performing, flailing, or striving in front of God, develop a rhythm of just sitting with Him.
- *Revamp your time with God.* Sometimes spending time with our Father feels like work because we treat it like work. So, throw out any expectations of what it's supposed to be like, and explore the opportunity of what it could be. Try a devotional, add in worship music, or change locations or the time of day.

- *Develop a rhythm of gratitude.* I try to list at least five things I'm grateful for each morning, and I intend to make sure I'm actually thanking God for those things—not just listing them blindly. Most people agree that practicing gratitude is essential, and most people don't have a rhythm for it in their daily lives. Noticing what God has done and is doing helps us fight discontent, bitterness, and defeat. Verbally thanking our Father helps us to feel more seen and connected to Him. It also sets us up for an entire day of watching to see God move.

- *Practice repentance.* Our souls will be continually exhausted if we don't take a moment to experience the thrill of repentance and the refreshment that comes after. So, confess to God, let the light of His love shine on the sin in your heart, and receive the grace that is yours for the taking.

- *Memorize Scripture to fight striving.* For the last fifteen years, I've been walking around muttering, "There is therefore now no condemnation for those in Christ Jesus," from Romans 8:1 (ESV). For many of us, memorizing Scripture might feel like one more task we must accomplish—let's don't do that. Instead, tuck a few key phrases in your mind to strike down the striving that comes when you want to perform for God or others. Here are a few suggestions: Psalm 46:10; John 15:3; Ephesians 2:8–9.

- *Develop a Sabbath rhythm.* Later in this chapter, we'll go into detail about Sabbath and how to develop a rhythm that works for you. Because you have done the work to find the places where you are most fatigued, you are now armed with the information to design a Sabbath that works for you. When I say it works for you, this has dual meaning. First, your Sabbath should be logistically attainable, and second, it should actually leave you feeling rested. I can't wait to dive into this with you.

Physical Rhythms

Only you can say for sure when it comes to your life, but for most of us, taking small steps to fight physical exhaustion would exponentially affect the other areas of our lives. For example, seeing what's happening in our spirits when our bodies are too tired is hard. Finding mental rest and peace when our bodies are tired is complicated. And it's almost impossible to stay emotionally stable when our bodies are tired.

So, I will share a list of increasingly in-depth rhythms, routines, and possibilities to fight physical exhaustion. Not every one will be right for you, and not every one will be accessible for your season. But try to fight the defeat that says none will work, and let's see what God can do. Here's one more reminder that we'd never try to conquer all of these at once—we'll take them one at a time to see lasting change in our lives.

Before I jump in, it's helpful to remind you that I am not a health care professional, and you should absolutely consult yours before making any shifts that would affect your mental or physical well-being in a negative way. That being said, I don't believe any of these will cause harm (I actually believe they'll all help)—but better safe than sorry.

- *Develop a bedtime routine that is calming and life-giving.* A bedtime routine signals to your body that it's time to relax and prepare for sleep. A bedtime routine is also scientifically proven to lower stress.[1]

- *Begin shutting down your phone or laptop a few hours before bed.* Exposure to blue light blocks the release of melatonin in our bodies.

- *Increase your daily water intake.* Dehydration impacts our circadian rhythm—the natural process in which our bodies and minds follow a twenty-four-hour pattern of wakefulness and sleep. Also, too much water close to bedtime will keep you up for other reasons! So, begin getting water earlier in the day.

- *Decrease your caffeine.* I am not trying to come for your coffee. I love coffee. That being said, it is a stimulant, and it profoundly affects our bodies. If we are continually struggling with exhaustion, yet we're unwilling to address our relationship with caffeine, it may be time to take another look. Even reducing the amount of coffee you drink and adjusting when you have it can have a positive effect on your physical fatigue.

- *See if you can increase your sleep window at night.* At the end of the day (that's a little pun for you), we all may need more actual time sleeping. It doesn't have to be a huge increase all at once. See if you can incrementally bump up your hours in bed over time. If you can't adjust when you wake up, begin by adjusting how early you head to bed. Even if you start with increments of five to ten minutes, that's a great place to begin.

- *Experiment with daily supplements.* Ideally, in a nonfallen world, we'd get every nutrient our body needs from our food and environment. But since we're not living in a perfect world, it can be incredibly beneficial for us to supplement our diets with additional vitamins and minerals. Hence supplements! Some of the most beneficial for physical exhaustion are vitamin B12, vitamin D, ashwagandha, fish oil, iron, and magnesium. In a perfect world, where health care weren't so hard for many of us, my most significant encouragement would be to get extensive blood work done to see where you have deficiencies. But if that isn't possible, talk to your doctor and use trial and error to see what helps.

- *Adjust your exercise rhythms.* Pull back if they're too strenuous or increase if you're more sedentary. Some studies show that the effects of aerobic exercise are similar to those of taking sleeping pills, but there is a point of diminishing returns. If you push your body too hard without rest days, overexercise can lead to insomnia.

- *Legs up the wall.* I started using this bio-hack almost every day. Scoot your seat up to the wall with your back on the ground for five to twenty minutes daily. Bring your legs straight up against the wall or slightly bent. This short exercise has a multitude of biological benefits. Even WebMD reports relaxation, stress relief, mind calming, and back pain relief as some of the benefits.[2]

- *Try taking small, quick catnaps during the day.* This one is not for everyone. It's certainly not for me. My husband can take a six-minute nap and wake up a new person. If I take a six-minute rest, I will wake up a new person too—but not someone you'd like to know. See if it works for you!

- Develop a routine of waiting before you say yes to opportunities. All the sleep hygiene in the world won't help if you're highly overcommitted during the day. Develop a bubble around your yes. Don't give it immediately. It will help you say no when the time is right.

- *Try getting sunlight directly on your skin first thing in the morning to set your circadian rhythm.* Our bodies' internal clocks are deeply impacted by light, and getting natural sunlight first thing in the morning alerts the rest of our internal systems that it's time to wake up. Waking them up right as we wake up gives us a better chance of allowing them to shut down fifteen hours later as we prepare for bed.

Mental Rhythms

All right, friends, now it's time to look at some rhythms that will help our beautiful brains get the rest they need. As always, these ideas are not for all at once, and they're not for everyone. So, try one rhythm, and try another if it's life-giving and reasonable for your schedule and responsibilities.

- *Create a morning routine.* In the same way that a nighttime routine trains and prepares our brains for sleep, a morning routine can prepare our minds for the day ahead. Play around with what works for you—a gratitude list, silence, drinking water, reading, stretching, and creativity. Fight the defeat that says it won't work for you, and don't believe the lie that your morning routine has to be more than a few minutes long.

   Even in hectic and shifting seasons, this can be a simple and effective habit to develop. A morning routine is nothing more than a pattern that works to prepare you for the day, so it could be as simple as taking a deep breath, reciting, "God loves me," and getting out of bed to start the day.

- *Engage in daily brain dumps.* A rhythm that has massively served me in the past is engaging in a "brain dump." I'll take a sheet of paper or even a whiteboard and list everything that overwhelms me, from small tasks to big, unsolvable questions. In fact, if anyone on my team feels overwhelmed, I love to do this rhythm together. This can also be great for couples.

- *Create a to-do list for the next day.* One factor that leaves us all feeling fatigued is the sense that we have so much more to get done and haven't finished it all. While I'm a firm believer that we'll never finish it all, having a list helps us shut down our brain when it's time to receive rest for the day. So, create a list for the next day, or even the next week, and then release that list to God.

- *Put limits on your phone.* Your phone is not the boss of you, but it will act like it if you let it. Your phone needs limits. It's not because you're weak but because the dopamine hit our brains receive from the notifications is real. So we have to work to retrain our responses. Here are a few ideas for setting limits on your phone: Put time limits on specific apps, turn off notifications, utilize Do Not Disturb or Airplane Mode for more extended periods when you need to be present, and delete apps that steal your time or attention during the week.

- *Clear spaces that are stressing you out.* Our eyes may adjust to clutter, but our brains often do not. If physical spaces in your life could use a little clearing, take a moment to love yourself and your brain well and tidy them up. I clean and straighten both my living room and my kitchen every morning and our team office before I begin work each day—nothing crazy or strenuous, just enough to make sure the spaces don't leave me unknowingly exhausted.

- *Take short walks to clear your head.* Your short walk could be around the parking lot of your office, to the mailbox, around the block with a stroller, or to the coffee shop for a little midday getaway. Taking a short walk helps our brain remember there's more to life than whatever was just in front of us. Nature often has a calming effect on our nervous system. And moving our body briefly helps our adrenal system work out stress and tension. Experiment with what works for your schedule, brain, and day.

- *Write and recite a prayer of release.* We talked about benevolent detachment in chapter 10. Practice this by developing a rhythm of reciting a prayer of release for particularly challenging areas of your life. If you find yourself stuck in a cycle of thinking, worrying, and obsessing, switch to reciting the prayer as much as you need it.

- *Plan the week and month ahead with intention.* Some of our mental fatigue can be counteracted with some intention and planning. If you don't have a rhythm for strategizing the days ahead, this may be a great time to start. Do this in community—with roommates, spouses, and others. Look at the calendar, discuss desires, and plan for margin and breaks when needed.

I love to start by writing down what I've already committed to do, or what I must do. This would be hours I need to be at work, times I need to pick up my kids, or moments where I've already committed to spend time in community. Then I schedule how and when I'll experience renewal, because if I don't plan those things intentionally, they won't happen. This would look like scheduling days off, workouts (because that's how I love to experience renewal), and a date night or two. Finally, I'll check to make sure that I've accounted for margin and transition time in my schedule.

Emotional Rhythms

You know the drill. Not all of these rhythms are for you, and none are meant to be attempted simultaneously. Pick what serves you and stick with it for a while.

- *Create a container for your feelings.* Whether it's a physical space, a physical time, or just a weekly rhythm where you let yourself let it all out—make room for your feelings, and invite God in.

- *Practice transitions well.* What often precludes us from feeling our feelings is transitioning to something else so quickly that we just move on. Pay attention to your transitions: Sit in the car to think over the day before going inside your home, make mental notes to return to, and do check-ins with yourself during massive transitions. It's also especially helpful to avoid screens during our transitions, even though it's become very normal to reach for them in margin moments. Take a breath and check in with your own emotions before receiving everything that threatens to pour through your phone and into your life.

- *Create a journaling practice.* The art of journaling is scientifically proven to have many emotional and physiological benefits. Explore ways to make it work: Journal in the Notes app on your phone or type on a laptop. Whatever you do, take a few moments and capture how you're feeling.

- *Find someone to process with.* In the back of this book, you'll find resources for therapists, counselors, and spiritual directors. Please know that there are many options for people in varying financial situations and life stages. Finding the right counselor or professional for you can take time, but it's worth the work.

A Word on Sabbath

By my count, we're about fifty thousand words into this book (so far), and we still haven't talked about the Sabbath. That's been intentional to some degree, but now it's time.

The idea of Sabbath fills many of us with a sense of obligation, defeat, and shame. It's just another thing we can't make happen or that we can't be good at. And while it's wildly important that we rewrite that narrative, I have so much compassion for those feelings because I've been there myself—and in so many ways, I still am.

My Sabbath practice is far from perfect. My husband and I obviously work on Sundays, so we're still in the tinkering process of figuring out what day works best for us to rest. I wish it were always standard and easy, but it's not—it's often complicated. We've been practicing Sabbath together intentionally for about eight years, and we still haven't nailed down exactly what works for us. And that makes sense because we are constantly evolving, as is our family.

Neither you nor I live in a Sabbath-centric culture. Most of us are not in Israel, where the rhythmic call to rest is embedded in culture. Even more problematic, many of our communities have cultures that praise busyness, hustle, and hurry. We have so much working against us. But let's see what Jesus has to say.

> One Sabbath day he was walking through a field of ripe grain. As his disciples made a path, they pulled off heads of grain. The Pharisees told on them to Jesus: "Look, your disciples are breaking Sabbath rules!"
>
> Jesus said, "Really? Haven't you ever read what David did when he was hungry, along with those who were with him? How he entered the sanctuary and ate fresh bread off the altar, with the Chief Priest Abiathar right there watching—holy bread that no one but priests were allowed to eat—and handed it out to his companions?" Then Jesus said, "The Sabbath was made to serve us; we weren't made to serve the Sabbath." (Mark 2:23–27 MSG)

Jesus said it best: The Sabbath is for us. It's a gift for us. In the same way that all rest is a gift for us. It is not a performance or a project that God is asking from us. Of course, there is a measure of faith and surrender in laying aside our work and striving to trust God. But even that worshipful sacrifice is for us, for our expressed intimacy and increased reliance on our Father.

Many of us are trying to build lives of obedience and worship while disobeying and ignoring this invitation to worship—the Sabbath. But Sabbath has never been about our righteousness or goodness; it's always been about His generosity and care for us.

One reason we get entirely hung up on the idea of Sabbath as a performance or a test we must pass is that we make the rules around it so incredibly religious and dogmatic. But here we see Jesus, with His disciples, "breaking the rules" and reminding them that the Sabbath is for us. It's not something we have to perfect.

And so I want to be succinct with my words and share my hope for you and me as we fight exhaustion on several different fronts.

The practice of Sabbath is perfectly designed as a gift from God to help us combat the physical, spiritual, mental, and emotional fatigue that has plagued us all our lives. It's a rhythm that takes time to develop, takes faith and trust to practice, and will cause us to go against the cultural flow of our communities. There will always be the temptation to make it dogmatic and legalistic, but we can combat that temptation by asking these questions and putting the answers into practice:

Can I take one day a week to enjoy God and His creation?

Can I take one day a week to trust God by not working?

Can I take one day a week to embrace rest and go against the culture of striving?

Which day of the week you pick, how you plan your day, and what you specifically try to do and don't do will be wildly different, varying from person to person and season to season. My encouragement is this: Find what works for you and remember that the Sabbath is for you. It is not something God wants from you.

If you are a mom who is physically exhausted from caring for others, I encourage you to find ways to physically rest when and where you can. Use disposable plates or let the dishes pile up. Don't do the laundry—just for one day. Forgo the nightly tidying of toys, say no to extracurricular activities for the evening if you're overstimulated and could use a quiet night.

If it's mental exhaustion that is weighing you down, take one day off from planning or strategizing. Close your laptop, capture complex thoughts, and ask God to help you release them. Better yet, leave your laptop in your office or turn your phone off completely.

If you find yourself emotionally exhausted, pay attention to how you engage with others and with media during your Sabbath. Maybe some lighthearted community time would do you good, or maybe you need to practice autonomy and enjoy some time by yourself. If you're emotionally exhausted, a great way to practice rest is by engaging the other facets of your life: Do something physical or mental. This will often give us a healthier outlet to process our emotions.

The great news about spiritual exhaustion is that it is usually fought by pursuing one thing: enjoying God. Do what helps you enjoy God, and remember you weren't created just to work for Him or make Him happy. Read a psalm that's brought you peace in the past, listen to a favorite old worship song, or just sit and talk to Him. Whatever you do, don't try to earn His favor or approval— and that includes trying to "Sabbath correctly."

For many of us, finding the right combination of activities (or lack of them) during our Sabbath will take time—but it's incredibly worth it. Communicating with the people in your life regarding your Sabbath and also receiving and hearing their desires will take intention. Every so often, if I'm noticing that our family is in need of a reset, I'll have a quick family meeting prior to our Sabbath. I'll ask what everyone's desires are, and we'll put together a plan that considers everyone as best as we can. And then I'll typically communicate something like this: "For my Sabbath, I'd like to *not plan*. So, after we establish our schedule, please help me to rest by not changing the plan, asking to create a new plan, or asking me what we'll eat/do/wear for the coming week. Thank you in advance!"

Whether it's spending time in nature, closing your laptop for the weekend, deleting social media from your phone, leaving the dishes and laundry, taking a break from studying, or asking your boss to have a conversation about more rhythmic days off from work, I know that developing your own Sabbath rhythm will take bravery and intention.

But I also know these two things: God is mighty in you, and Sabbath is worth it.

Some final thoughts on Sabbath:

I think, as a society, we spend the bulk of our energy where Sabbath is concerned playing devil's advocate. But I've never been particularly keen on being the enemy's advocate—you know?

There is a lie that says, "This will never work for you. No one understands your circumstances or the pressure you're under. It must be nice for those who can afford to take a Sabbath, but for real people this is totally unattainable."

My question for you is this: Whose voice does that sound like? Does it sound like your Father, who loves you and wants rest for you, who sees your value outside of what you can produce? Or does it sound like the enemy of your soul? The one who will do whatever it takes to steal your rest, kill your peace, and destroy your intimacy with God and others. The enemy has the most to gain from you continuing on in a narrative that leaves you isolated, exhausted, and feeling out on a limb.

Get Back on the Horse

Please picture me coming as close to you as you're physically comfortable with as I tell you what may be the most important thing I have said so far in this chapter.

Be ready to get back on the horse. Because, unfortunately, the fall is inevitable for all of us.

You will also fail as you reset your rhythms, embrace moments and routines of rest, fight exhaustion, and strive and work yourself to the bone. You're going to fall out of rhythm. You'll have a busy week and drop all your healthy practices. You're going to mess up. But then, you'll get back on the horse and try again.

Don't wallow in shame, don't beat yourself up, and don't decide that you're over it and you're never going to rest again. Instead, just get back on the horse and try again. It's worth it.

fourteen

change the culture

Every woman I know is tired, but every woman I know is loved by a God who *wants* rest for them. What if we stopped living in reactive defeat, accepting exhaustion as our way of life? What if, starting with us, we broke ties with the glorification of busy and the idolization of a toil-filled life? What if we defiantly and worshipfully started honoring our own limitations, boundaries, and borders? And what if *all of that* was so compelling that it started a wave in our communities?

My prayer is that you feel less tired when you implement some of the shifts in this book. I want your life to actually feel different when you close this book and keep getting more aligned with the kingdom of God. I know you'll keep experiencing physical, spiritual, mental, and emotional fatigue because you'll keep living on this earth under the effects of a fallen world. But I pray that this book helps you feel more equipped to react and respond worshipfully, resisting the pull to keep pushing until you collapse or can't care anymore.

And because I want you to actually feel better, this entire chapter is about involving and engaging your community. Because one woman fighting fatigue is beautiful, but a whole community shifting the way they talk, move, serve, and live—that will change the world. Plus, I want you to have pals along the way. So, if you haven't already, here's my encouragement to take a quick picture of the cover of this book and text a friend. You can even just take a picture of the sentence below because I want to make it as easy as possible for you:

> Hey, friend! Have you read or heard of this book, *Tired of Being Tired*? I'd like to talk to you about it. Maybe grab a copy right now, or you can borrow mine when I'm done. Sound OK?

Good job! Wasn't that easy? OK, now let's talk about how to pull in your people in Jesus's name.

Change the Language

I blink back tired tears as I drive to church. I'm too tired to yawn, too tired to think. I really needed more sleep this morning, but who doesn't? This is what we do. This is what we're supposed to do on Sundays. *Maybe I can nap later*, I think, but then I remember I have my cousin's baby shower to attend. The rest of my family is out of town, so it's pretty crucial that I show up to represent.

This is exactly why I'm headed into church this morning, to represent and show up. Not necessarily to be seen, but most definitely to do my part in seeing others. I'll get some rest . . . tonight. Hopefully.

I chastise myself for inwardly groaning as I see the woman volunteering to hold the door open as I approach. I can't even really remember her name because my brain is mush these days, but she always knows mine. She's always here. She's everywhere. And she has the trail of perfect kids, the perfect hair, and the cutest outfits I've ever seen. And I'm walking in eight minutes late with a coffee stain and under eyelids that look bruised from the bags weighing them down.

After she asks how I'm doing, I ask it back, fulfilling the obligation, and she begins to run down a list of all her family had going on this week. Somehow, without her saying anything overtly hurtful or prideful, I walk away feeling smaller and weaker than I did before I walked in. Her life is so busy, tidy, and happy, and mine is so frantic. I feel like I must be doing too much and should be doing more all at once. *What's wrong with me?* I think, as I look for an empty seat in the worship center.

Have you ever noticed how much defeated acceptance of our exhaustion we find in small talk? We love to talk about how busy, fatigued, and overworked we are. Whether it's at church, when we run into acquaintances around town, or even when we're catching up with family and friends—it seems inevitable.

"Life is good! Busy, but good!"

"Ha! What's a vacation? Must be nice!"

"I thrive on five hours of sleep a night."

"You can have it all. You just have to figure out how to fit it all in."

"I haven't had a day off in weeks. But you know how it is!"

"I'll sleep when I'm dead."

"I'm a people pleaser. It's just who I am."

We build our worlds with words. And the words we use about our capacity, energy, rest, and pace are undeniably shifting the individuals and communities around us. In the same way, the words we're hearing, receiving, and absorbing are also affecting us.

If you've struggled to make real and lasting shifts to your life, the community around you likely has not been receptive to growth in this area. So, how do we change the culture? How do we help everyone else get so tired of being tired that they start embracing the rest God has for them? We must change our language regarding our fatigue to see lasting change in our communities and personal lives. We have to change the language to change the culture.

Here's the good news: We have so much power to change the language because we get to pick the words we use in community. One woman shifting how she talks about her fatigue, pace, purpose, emotions, and mental capacity will impact the people around her. You will impact the community you're in, in Jesus's name.

I'd love to share a few ways to start with ourselves to shift the language and culture. See if any of these would be meaningful for you and the people you do life with:

- *No more glorifying busy or tired.* This change starts inwardly for most of us as God changes our minds. But we can come into agreement with a kingdom pace by not humblebragging about how tired or full our days are. We should not be proud of this, especially if we know we're living outside the boundaries and borders of the capacity God has given us. We can also be cautious not to praise the tired and busy around us but to show compassion toward them.

- *No more self-identifying as people pleasers.* Struggling with people-pleasing is a natural and understandable tension. But as worshipers of God and followers of Jesus, we can't make this our identity and claim it as if it were positive. People-pleasing does not make us good servants and leaders; it makes us idol worshipers, and it will absolutely lead to a life that is exhausting on multiple levels.

- *No more apologizing for saying no, needing rest, or setting boundaries.* We should say sorry when we're wrong or hurt someone—intentionally or not. But I don't believe we should apologize for needing rest, which would be apologizing for how God made us. And I also don't think we should apologize for not meeting someone else's unhealthy expectations of our capacity. It will initially feel awkward, but cut the *sorry* out of your boundary-setting and see your community change forever.

- *No more glossing over how bad your exhaustion really is.* I'm not advocating that you spill your guts to a stranger or acquaintance about your fatigue. But among our closest friends, in our most intimate relationships, we have to be honest about how we're doing. If you're physically, spiritually, mentally, and emotionally exhausted—your people need to know. Unfortunately, many of us are suffering silently, without hope, because no one who loves us knows how tired we are. It's time to change that.

Here's the excellent news: Changing the language does work. It creates an atmosphere where others can dip their toes into the life-changing water of embracing realistic rest. And while it will require you to be courageously honest, it's an investment that will continually give back to you as you see your culture shift.

It's time to change the language around rest. So, let's start with us.

Change the Pace

I tell people settling at Bright City, our church in Charleston, there's one thing they need to know before they fully commit: The best thing about Bright City is the pace, and the worst thing about Bright City is the pace.

Here's what I mean: We're working in a post-Christian, post-megachurch context, where many of the people who own the mission are coming back to God after some form of deconstruction, church hurt, or time away from the family of God. And the thing about people returning to church is that they don't want to be rushed. They don't want anything overly programmed. They can't be hyped into participation. And I love this about our people.

So, that means that the pace of our church is relatively slow. We don't have a million things scheduled. We don't have a ton of ministries. We've got groups and kids' ministry, and that's about it. Everything else is organic. We take multiple Sundays off a year to give our volunteers and staff time to rest. We'll let a service get full before adding another one. It's beautiful, and I love it. Personally, even for me—someone who is very often at everything we host as a church—I never feel like I have to go to church; I feel like I get to. It still feels like a privilege, not an obligation.

But there's a downside to this too. When someone has a fantastic ministry or event idea and we don't perceive that we have the margin to do it well, we say no. There is a small contingency of people who do not like that we take "Sabbath Sundays," or days off from gathering for corporate worship. And I get that too. But I hold the bigger picture and know we're in this for the long haul. We're building a family. And a family needs time to get to know one another and figure out who they are. If we rush that process, people will burn out and leave, and the family will suffer. So I warn them: You'll love the pace, and sometimes you won't love it so much.

For us to see lasting change in our communities and, therefore, our own lives, we'll have to have a collective shift in our pace. I find that it's hard enough to incorporate rhythms of rest in our lives when we add other people—the wheels come off. It just feels like the more people you add to an equation, the more frantic and rushed it often becomes. But there are ways we can pump the brakes in our relationships and work together to change the pace. Here are a few ideas for you:

- *Give things time and space to grow organically.* One of the spaces in which I see a frenetic pace enter communities is the development of relationships. We feel the need to connect as soon as possible in a deep and meaningful way, when a more organic evolution is often healthier in the long haul.

210

Simply put, fast-formed friendships can often be the most exhausting. Give yourself and others time to get to know one another.

- *Decide corporately that not every good idea is God's idea.* Friends, if I had to say yes to every good idea I've had with a friend, I would have tried to start an airline (true story— horrible idea), bought my friend's business (that I knew nothing about), and moved to Manhattan on a whim. I love a fun idea that we come up with together, but one of the most important ways I can fight exhaustion is by acknowledging that not every good, fun, or exciting idea is necessarily from God. Having relationships in which we can get excited and throw out ideas without acting on them is the definition of maturity.

- *Normalize different paces in different seasons.* In this book, we've spoken a good bit about embracing different needs for rest in varying seasons, but this deserves a moment here as we discuss community. When women develop or even settle into a rhythm or pattern of community, there's a natural anticipation for that to continue, when sometimes it can't. Sometimes we're in a season of seeing one another daily, and that's beautiful, and sometimes a once-a-quarter catch-up with a good friend is the best we can muster. To truly see our communities become less collectively exhausted, we have to keep the lines of communication open about our current needs and capacity.

Invite, Don't Incite

It's human nature to learn something and immediately want to share it with everyone we know. We can't help it. You've probably done it multiple times throughout this book. We hear a sermon, see a social media post, read a book, and think, *Wow. So-and-so really struggles with this. I wish they'd read this.* It's natural. It happens. But we've got some options about how we want to handle this phenomenon.

I'm willing to bet that at some point—if not many points—during this introspective look into your own life, you've identified how it would be easier to fight fatigue if so-and-so didn't do

_____.

If your husband didn't schedule a guys' night so often without asking.

If your mom didn't have such demanding expectations of how often you'll connect.

If your boss didn't push the limits of the workweek so aggressively.

If your pastor or ministry leader didn't expect so much.

If your friend wasn't going through such a hard time.

If your kids weren't in so many sports.

If your friend group didn't seem so dead set against sharing real feelings.

My encouragement here is short and straightforward: Invite, don't incite.

Use the curious compassion that you've allowed for yourself in order to be gentle with the people in your life who are "bad at rest." Don't judge where they're at and incite condemnation or pride. Instead, invite them into the fresh truths you've been discovering. Invite them into change rather than inciting their shame because they don't know it all yet.

We only know what we know now because our good and kind Father has let us know it. So, if the people in your community are behind in learning healthy ways to battle their fatigue, we can choose patience for them while breaking ties with the unhealthy rhythms in our own life.

But one incredible way we can see the culture shift is by inviting the people we love (or really want to love) into the freedom we're pursuing from fatigue in our lives. We can lovingly and patiently start conversations about the kinds of exhaustion our people are fighting. We can make space to listen as they process and grieve their tiredness. We can ask questions about where they're at, how they got there, and where they want to go regarding their own rest.

Here are a few starter questions to help you broach these conversations:

- I've heard you say recently that you're tired. Do you want to talk about it?
- Where do you feel like the bulk of your fatigue is coming from?
- I've recently been on a journey to fight my own fatigue. Would you want to hear more?

And we can invite them into new ways, places, and paths to rest. But we will lose them if we come toward them trying to incite change with judgment or provocation. People may experience short-term change when they experience shame, but it will never bring the lasting fruit our communities are desperate for.

Your people, your friends, your family—they're so incredibly influenced by you. And it's not your responsibility to change their minds or lives, but it can be your honor to invite them into something new and healthy. Then you get the joy of seeing healing and refreshment come to their lives—and you have an ally in the fight against fatigue. You will have a partner or many to help you stay on the path when hurrying, striving, and distracted living threaten to make you settle for tired. You aren't alone now, but you won't even feel alone when you invite others to join you on this journey.

You are a culture changer, a world shifter, a woman who takes the rest God gives her and encourages others in the same way.

fifteen

He gives rest to those He loves

The paradox of this book is that embracing rest will always feel unfinished because it is such a messy, ongoing business. I don't think you should trust people who preach a one-dimensional, clear-cut path to fighting fatigue, because rest could not be further from one-dimensional or clear-cut. Our lives are wild, messy, mysterious, spiritual, mundane, and sacred. Our lives are not simple, so our path to rest will always look more like a nature hike and less like a stroll through a manicured park.

That being said, there's one last thing I want to make sure we both agree with before our time together is done:

God gives rest to those He loves.

And He loves you.

So, when you wonder if you deserve it, remind your heart that you could never earn His compassion—but He gives rest to those He loves.

When you're tempted to keep everything as it's been and stay tired so you don't ruffle feathers, remind your heart that you don't want to eschew His good gift—and He gives rest to those He loves.

When you're worried that you were a little extra, and maybe you got too hyped about this whole idea, remind your heart that no one is more passionate about our energy than God—and He gives rest to those He loves.

When things get wild again, and all your rhythms are out of whack, remind your heart that God's kingdom comes when His will is done—and He gives rest to those He loves.

I'm fascinated by John and Charles Wesley, two of the most notable evangelists and church fathers of the 1700s, who were also brothers. They played a significant role in Christian life: John is credited with being the founder of the Methodist church, and Charles worked alongside him, writing over 6,500 hymns, many of which the church still sings today.

In college, Charles founded a small group of men seeking the "holiness of heart and life," which others outside the group would call "the Holy Club."[1] These men met together several times a week and devoted themselves to walking with God. They prayed together, studied the Word together, served people experiencing poverty together, and developed a set of questions to check in on their souls rhythmically in community.

The rumored story of the twenty-two questions goes like this: The men would ask one another upon meeting, "Is your heart burning for Jesus?" And if someone could not say yes or testify to burning devotion, they'd work through this set of questions to see where there was a potential lack of connection with God.[2] The questions are beautiful for self-reflection, and after hearing this story, I began keeping them in the front of my journal. I receive them not as hypervigilant accountability but as helpful guides to be curious about how I'm receiving what God has for me. I won't share them all here, but these are a few of my favorites for reference:

- Did the Bible live in me today?
- Do I insist upon doing anything about which my conscience is uneasy?
- Am I defeated in any part of my life?

Here's what I'm wondering: Could you and I—could we, a collective of women who are tired of being tired—start our own club? Could we enter into an agreement that we want to live as daughters of God, not exhausted women who live like this is all there is for us? Should we call it the "Awake Women's Club"?

If you're in, if you'd like to join, the entrance requirements won't demand that you change every part of your life all at once. Likewise, joining this club won't mean that you have to withdraw from community or become someone entirely different. Rather, we'll just move through our lives, searching our hearts and evaluating our rhythms to determine, *Am I living like God gives rest to those He loves? Am I receiving what God has for me rather than sleepwalking spiritually, physically, emotionally, and mentally?*

To end our time together and begin the rest of our messy, miraculous journeys toward more rested living, I have a set of questions for us to ask. Maybe you want to write them in the front of your journal or tape them to your bathroom mirror. My prayer is that utilizing them doesn't feel like condemnation but rather an invitation to examine whether you're living fully awake to God's love.

Let's dive in together.

1. Am I currently tired, and if so, in what way?
2. How do I perceive God's posture toward me and my exhaustion?
3. Am I trying to push through my fatigue in ways God has not asked me to?
4. Am I feeling shame or pride about my level of fatigue?
5. Does my heart feel spiritually tired?
6. Am I trying to earn God's approval or affection?
7. Is the gospel still real to me?
8. Is my body physically tired?
9. Am I pushing myself past my physical limits to prove something to myself or others?
10. Do I believe I am more responsible than God in any situation?

11. Is my mind tired?
12. Am I making space for silence, solitude, and mental rest?
13. Do I still believe in the miraculous power of peace that passes understanding?
14. Am I emotionally exhausted?
15. Have I made space to process my emotions with myself and God?
16. Are there any feelings weighing down my spirit that require confession, wisdom, or action on my part?
17. Are my daily rhythms reflecting a life of grace, peace, and God's goodness?
18. Am I inviting others into rhythms of rest with me?
19. Do I want to keep living exhausted, or do I want to see change in my life?
20. Do I believe God gives rest to those He loves?

My prayer for you is that if you enter in and ask any of these questions, none of them will be about having the "right" answer or doing the "right" thing. I pray that you'll feel God's love and compassion in your presence, and His grace will compel you to an honest answer that leads to deeper intimacy.

I'm so incredibly grateful that you were tired enough of being tired to pick up this book. I'm so incredibly grateful that you came with me through stories, Bible verses, and unceremonious metaphors to take a deeper look at why we got to this place and how we can move forward.

But what's next is entirely up to you.

If you've made it this far, I have a feeling you'll never go back to accepting a life of tiredness. I have a feeling you'll never again blindly choose busy, distracted, defeated, and exhausted living just because it's easier. I have a feeling you'll fight to stay fully awake.

My promise to you is this: I will too.

I'm with you. God is with you. And He gives rest to those He loves.

acknowledgments

Father, I thank You for loving me enough to chase me during all the years I ran from rest.

Jenni Burke and Stephanie Smith, I cannot believe I've gotten to write so many books with the two of you as my midwives. Thanks for letting me sit in a conference room in Michigan and cry about how tired I was. I think God used that day in a mighty way. Jenni—thank you for believing in this message before anyone else. Stephanie—thank you for making it what it is.

Rebekah Guzman and Kristin Adkinson—thank you for your careful and curious editing. Knowing wise women like you have my back enables me to be brave.

Mark Rice, Eileen Hanson, and the rest of the team at Baker—there is no one like you in the publishing world. You are all generous, kingdom-minded, reader-focused, and you make my job a dream come true.

John Mark McMillan—thanks for the *Live at the Knight* album. It's been the soundtrack to every book I've written, but for this one in particular, I needed those songs in my ears to get the words out of my head.

To the team and every single coach at Go + Tell Gals—this is for us. I never worry if we'll be "successful" (whatever that means);

I only worry we won't rest. But I'll stop worrying now that we've all joined this club.

Aspen and Hampton—I know I didn't get to birth you beautiful gals, but I got to watch your respective moms bring you into this world as I wrote this book. I was thinking about you, praying for you, and cooing over you every day that I sat down to type. You're the future and the world changers, and we can't wait to see what God does in your lives. Hug your moms—they are both incredible and mean everything to me.

Mom, Katie, and Caroline—thank you for boat rides, text threads, angels to the NSEW, dark back porches, road trips, friendships, and being my family. I love you so much.

Connolly kids—this is a thank-you and an apology. I'm sorry for how long it took me to get tired of being tired. I pray the rest of your lives you find me and your dad a soft place to land.

Nick Connolly—this book, more than any other I've written, is inspired by you. You've always lived a kingdom pace; I'm just trying to keep up (slow down). Thank you.

resources

Spiritual Direction

The Transforming Center:
> Features spiritual directors you can meet with virtually all over the United States, as well as retreats and other resources, TransformingCenter.org.

Therapy

Faithful Counseling:
> Online Christian counseling, FaithfulCounseling.com.

Onsite:
> In-person and online workshops and retreats that help with personal growth and emotional wellness, OnsiteWorkshops.com.

Open Path Psychotherapy Collective:
> Open Path connects clients in need with mental health professionals who offer affordable therapy, OpenPathCollective.org.

notes

Chapter 1 Our Exhaustion Runs Deep

1. Kim Elsesser, "Women Are Suffering from an 'Exhaustion Gap' according to New Study," *Forbes*, March 14, 2022, https://www.forbes.com/sites/kimelsesser /2022/03/14/women-are-suffering-from-an-exhaustion-gap-according-to-new -study/?sh=6ac6db137b3a.

2. Seema Khosla, "Restful Night's Sleep More Likely for Men than Women," HealthDay, May 20, 2022, https://consumer.healthday.com/b-5-20-restful-night -s-sleep-more-likely-for-men-than-women-2657336717.html.

Chapter 5 Spiritual Exhaustion: "I just need to get through the next few weeks."

1. C. S. Lewis, *The Joyful Christian* (New York: Simon and Schuster, 1996), 138.

Chapter 7 Physical Exhaustion: "I can't just quit."

1. Timothy Keller, *How to Reach the Christian West: Six Essential Ingredients of a Missionary Encounter* (New York: Redeemer City-to-City, 2020), 30.

2. Keller, *How to Reach the Christian West*, 30.

Chapter 9 Mental Exhaustion: "My brain is fried."

1. David Burkus, "Research Shows That Organizations Benefit When Employees Take Sabbaticals," *Harvard Business Review*, August 10, 2017, https:// hbr.org/2017/08/research-shows-that-organizations-benefit-when-employees-take -sabbaticals.

2. Burkus, "Organizations Benefit When Employees Take Sabbaticals."

3. Ruth Haley Barton, *Invitation to Solitude and Silence: Experiencing God's Transforming Presence* (Westmont, IL: IVP, 2009), 29.

4. Dr. Caroline Leaf, *Switch On Your Brain: The Key to Peak Happiness, Thinking, and Health* (Grand Rapids: Baker Books, 2015), 93–94.

5. *The West Wing*, season 3, episode 11, "H. Con-172," directed by Vincent Misiano, written by Aaron Sorkin, Eli Attie, and Felicia Willson, featuring Rob Lowe, Dulé Hill, and Allison Janney, aired January 9, 2002, on NBC.

Chapter 10 Mental Exhaustion: "Peace is my birthright."

1. This is a variation of the wording in the ESV.

2. John Eldredge, *Get Your Life Back: Everyday Practices for a World Gone Mad* (Nashville: Thomas Nelson, 2020), 16.

3. Eldredge, *Get Your Life Back*, 16.

Chapter 12 Emotional Exhaustion: "I am loved and cared for."

1. Emily Nagoski and Amelia Nagoski, *Burnout: The Secret to Unlocking the Stress Cycle* (New York: Random House, 2019).

Chapter 13 Reset Your Rhythms

1. Danielle Pacheco and Heather Wright, "Bedtime Routines for Adults," Sleep Foundation, updated June 23, 2023, https://www.sleepfoundation.org/sleep-hygiene/bedtime-routine-for-adults.

2. Martin Taylor, "What to Know about Legs-Up-the-Wall Yoga Pose," Jump Start by WebMD, reviewed by Jabeen Begum, MD, November 11, 2021, https://www.webmd.com/fitness-exercise/what-to-know-legs-up-wall-yoga-pose.

Chapter 15 He Gives Rest to Those He Loves

1. Joe Iovino, "The Method of Early Methodism: The Oxford Holy Club," United Methodist Communications, September 20, 2016, https://www.umc.org/en/content/the-method-of-early-methodism-the-oxford-holy-club.

2. Iovino, "Method of Early Methodism."

Jess Connolly

is the author of several books, including
You Are the Girl for the Job and _Breaking Free from Body Shame_, and coauthor
of _Wild and Free_. She and her husband,
Nick, planted Bright City Church in
Charleston, South Carolina, where they
live with their four children. As the lead
coach and founder of Go + Tell Gals
and the host of _The Jess Connolly Podcast_, Jess wants to leave her generation
more in awe of God than she found it.
She's passionate about her family, discipling women, God's Word, and the local
church.

·······Connect with Jess········

JessConnolly.com

Jess Connolly

JessAConnolly

JessAConnolly